LIFE & TRADITION IN THE YORKSHIRE DALES

Happy Anniversary 1977
Here's to the next 27 years!
luv — Sue 'n John

LIFE & TRADITION
in the
YORKSHIRE DALES

by MARIE HARTLEY
and JOAN INGILBY

with 261 photographs
14 pages of drawings
and a map

LONDON: J. M. DENT & SONS LTD

Made in Great Britain
at the
Aldine Press · Letchworth · Herts
for
J. M. DENT & SONS LTD
Aldine House · Albemarle Street · London
First published 1968
Reprinted 1968, 1969, 1973

ISBN: 0 460 03807 9

CONTENTS

PHOTOGRAPHS

vii

DRAWINGS

Swaledale saying: 'Riving t' world
off its crooks.' (Working hard.)

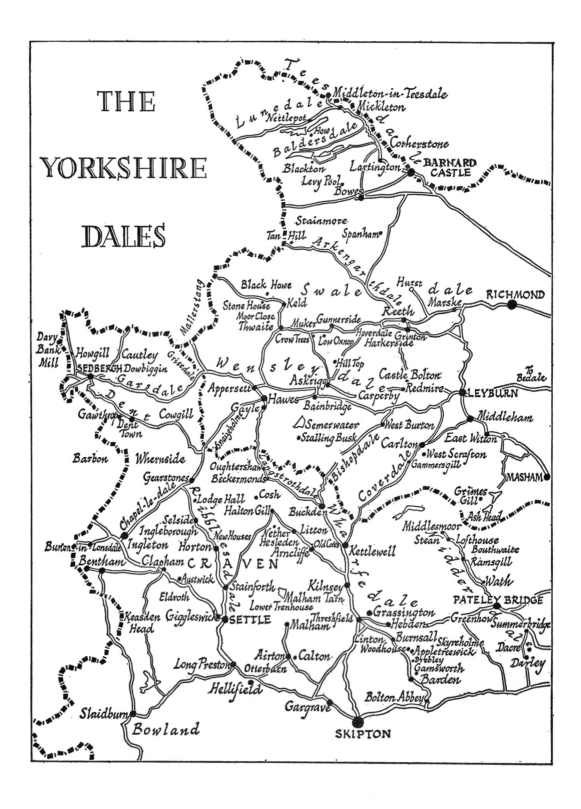

THE

YORKSHIRE

DALES

FOREWORD

& ACKNOWLEDGMENTS

IN the area of this study—the hill country of the Yorkshire dales—a similar tradition of pastoral farming, building in stone, and domestic practices prevails throughout the whole region. Yet, within it there are the slight regional variations likely to be found in areas cut off from each other by barriers of hills. The main disparity is between the dales in the West Riding (the Craven dales) and those in the North Riding, where for example different breeds of sheep and nuances in dialect are found. Farming and domestic practices vary from one dale to another, as witness the types of peat spade peculiar to each dale and the different kinds of oatcake baked there. But with these qualifications it is true to say that the dales are a homogeneous whole, exhibiting a similar history and a background of relentless depopulation throughout the last hundred years.

The study of a region is inevitably related to the period in which it is written—in this case a period of transition, bridging the gap between the old life of farm, village and market town which had been pursued for centuries, and life at the present day with its breakdown in traditional practices.

The change has been taking place with ever increasing momentum since the invention of machines began to make itself felt. It has been accelerated by depopulation; it became marked at the time of the First World War when, with the already prevalent mass production of consumer goods, the village craftsman continued his downhill slide to almost but not quite total extinction; it came with a rush following the Second World War when the horse, already well on its way to complete replacement by the motor car on the roads, was superseded by tractors on the farm. Age-old practices in farming, which had been slowly seeping away, have gone during the last ten years—gone with extraordinary speed.

In the past it is true, men worked like machines; the saddlers stitching at their leather, the scythemen mowing across a field, to mention two examples. 'It was all work i' them days.' 'It had all to come from your finger ends,' are the cries. 'Owt widn't deu' is added, meaning that every practice in farming and craft had to be undertaken in a correct and orderly manner.

It is true too, that financial recompense was not commensurate with endeavour.

By present day standards the stone walls were built by sweated labour. Cake once a week, and jam or butter, not both, on bread was the rule. Many farmers subsisted on a similar level on small farms, whose amalgamation to make larger holdings has been accelerated during the last twenty years. Yet, whilst it remained full and vigorous, life in the dales' villages offered pride in work and simple pleasures.

It was part of the economy to be self-sufficient and to make use of all that was to hand. Craftsmen made many of their own tools as necessity dictated. On the moors, peat was cut for fuel, rushes were gathered for bedding and for stripping to obtain the pith for wicks for rush-lights, whilst ling was pulled for lighting fires, for making besoms and for thatching houses. Cows' horns were utilized as containers for holding medicine for dosing cattle, for keeping stone-flies for fishing, for carrying grease for *strickles* (sharpening tools for scythes) and for blowing a blast on to call the cattle at milking time.

So much was interrelated. When most of the gentry and the professional classes left the upper dales, the craftsmen lost their best customers, and when the craftsmen went the roots of life in the villages and market towns were loosened.

Any recording now of the old life as it slips away, is only just in the nick of time. Because farming in the dales is different from that elsewhere, we have given considerable detail of farming practices, but because there exist specialist books on individual crafts we have usually omitted craft methods. Except where it impinges upon rural life, we have ignored industry such as lead-mining, which already has a literature of its own.

When in the summer of 1965 our friends at Stone House, upper Swaledale, left the farm, they gave us a considerable collection of farming bygones, which, added to those we had collected over a period of twenty years, have formed an invaluable background to this book. Also our work was eased initially by the many friends in the dales to whom we knew we could turn for assistance. We have talked to and photographed many people, to whom we owe gratitude. In order not to repeat their names here, we especially thank all those mentioned in the text and those who figure in the photographs. We are also indebted to: Mrs J. Alderson (senior) and family, Mr and Mrs W. Alderson, Mr G. K. Benson, Mr P. Calvert, Miss M. Capstick, Mr and Mrs F. Caton, Mr and Mrs Calvert Chapman, Mr R. M. Chapman, Mr E. Cooper, Mr E. Dinsdale, Miss F. Garth, Miss H. Hawkswell, Mr and Mrs R. M. Hodgson, Mr R. H. Hunter, Mr W. Marwood, Mr and Mrs T. Maudsley, Mr R. Metcalfe, Mr and Mrs H. Moon, Mr and Mrs J. Morphet, Mr J. R. Morphet, Miss J. B. D. Radford, Mr J. Redmayne, Mr J. Scarr, Mr and Mrs J. R. Smith, Dr H. Thistlethwaite and Mr and Mrs E. Walker. We have talked to many other people who are so numerous that we can only thank them all.

Besides these we have had help from the curators of the Bowes Museum,

Barnard Castle; the Welsh Folk Museum, St Fagan's Castle, Cardiff; the Museum of English Rural Life, Reading; National Museum of Antiquities of Scotland, Edinburgh; and the Public Library and Museum, Skipton; and private collectors: Mr Tom Lord of Settle and Mr R. Tyson of Leyburn.

Lastly, most of the photographs have been taken by the authors in the years 1965–1967, and all of these are of genuine activities, except those specially posed for us, which are plates 26, 29, 41, 85–88, 112–16, 141, 214, 217, 224–7, 258, 259. Where the photographs are self-explanatory, there is no accompanying text.

We wish to thank Mrs N. Dyson for obtaining the photograph for plate 18, *The Dalesman* for the loan of the block for plate 48, and the following for the photographs for the plates as numbered: *Northern Echo*, 21; Mr K. Shepherd, 52, 89, 104, 105, 119, 252; Mr B. Unné, 46, 98, 99, 184, 213, 218, 219, 220; Mr R. Haygarth, 163; Dr J. A. Farrer, 199, 200, 201, 202; Mr G. Hare, 211; *The Yorkshire Post*, 245. We also thank for the loan of old photographs: Mr J. E. Metcalfe, 2 (wash drawing); Mrs W. H. Nixon, 19, 20, 191; Mrs H. Verity, 74; Mr W. G. Wallbank, 75, 91; Mr G. K. Benson, 89; Mrs I. Harrison and Miss S. Caton, 92; Mr R. Tyson, 93, 250; Mrs G. B. Porter, 96; Mr F. Shields, 97; Mr T. Lord, 103, 248; Mr R. B. Fawcett, 102; Mr J. and Mr R. Wallbank, 109, 110; Mr T. Hayward, 143; Mr W. Blakey, 142; Mr G. Hare, 145, 211, 243; Mr C. Chapman, 146, 168; the late Mr W. Calvert, 167; Mr Tom Peacock, 244; Mr W. H. Walker, 249; Mrs T. Taylor, 216; Bankfield Museum, Halifax, 231; Mrs G. E. Sedgwick, 233; Mr W. J. Blades, 247.

FARMHOUSES, FIREPLACES
& FURNISHINGS

MOST of the sites of the farmhouses of the Yorkshire Dales are ancient. Determined by the proximity to water, they stand close to becks or springs; many still have shallow wells fed from springs in back kitchens. Some originated as manor houses or small halls but none of this class retains the medieval hall plan except High Hall, Appletreewick, whose hall with upper floor, simple type of screens passage and gallery derives from this. Some occupy the sites of monastic granges and possess early features. A circular staircase, now blocked up, at Old Cotes, Littondale (1650), is sited as in fifteenth-century plans at the side of the porch. Other farmhouses, of which a few are in Nidderdale, exhibit the early wooden framework of pairs of crucks; but these are rare in the dales.

In general, the ancient structural arrangements have largely disappeared, erased by rebuildings and reconstructions taking place onwards from the sixteenth and seventeenth centuries (when stone replaced wood as a building material) until almost the present day.

Externally but not internally, innumerable farmhouses retain the traditional plan of the long house in which house and cow shed, adjoining under one roof, were open to each other or connected by a door. But often now the hay mow not the cow shed is next to the house. Farmhouses such as Kepp House, Burton-in-Lonsdale and Crow Trees, Cowan Bridge, on the borders of Yorkshire and Lancashire, approximate to the plan of the long house in that formerly they had doors opening immediately from the kitchen into the *fodder gang* of the cow shed. At Scar House, upper Swaledale, a farmhouse has access across a passage from back kitchen to cow house, and in 1965 we found workmen blocking up a doorway which had the same arrangement at Ruecrofts, Howgill, near Sedbergh. This house, reconstructed in the eighteenth century, has a beef loft, a buttery and, until recently, had a bakstone for baking *haverbread*.

In areas of strong Norse occupation as late as the seventeenth century, a farmhouse was known as a 'seat house,' a term harking back to the summer house of the Norsemen and to the practice of transhumance.[1] However, a more general term for the farmhouse is 'fire house' which occurs in many Elizabethan and Stuart deeds. Defining a building with a fire as opposed to the cow shed, it reminds us of the medieval arrangement of a central hearth in the middle of the room with a hole in the roof for the escape of smoke.

When the central hearth was moved to a gable wall, the tradition was continued in the central chimney stack to be seen in some yeomen's houses of the seventeenth century: Worton Hall, Wensleydale (1600), Woodhouse Manor, Wharfedale, Lumb Farm, Settle (1702), Low Oxnop, Swaledale (1685) and West New House, Bishopdale (1635). In these, the kitchen and parlour fireplaces are back to back on either side of a thick wall containing a wide flue.

Houses of this date constitute the most interesting farmhouses of the dales and are characterized by mullion windows, dated door-heads and stone arches which framed an open hearth with firedogs. In many, the space under the arch formed an inglenook, and the space above has been open and was boxed off in the bedroom above. From the *galley-bauk* or *reckan-bauk*, a bar in the chimney, an iron chain was suspended from which hung a *reckan-crook* (pot-hook), or a crane supporting reckan-crooks was fixed on the fire back. Alongside several of these fireplaces is a small side arch through which the parlour was reached, or it formed a cupboard or possibly contained a circular staircase to the first floor. But mostly, staircases were accommodated in an outshut at the back of the house.

In the Middle Ages many villages had communal ovens, often housed in separate buildings and often resembling in shape small igloos. Such ovens are still to be seen outside village houses in Asia Minor. In 1218, Bainbridge in Wensleydale, then a new model village, had a common oven. Until the replacement by cast-iron ovens many individual houses had a brick or beehive oven, as it is called from the shape of the interior. Most were built into the thickness of the wall, usually near the fireplace; some projected externally. We have found nineteen of them in the dales, some intact, some partially blocked up, some altogether plastered over. Few iron doors survive. Some have no flue; others a slit-like opening immediately above the door, and in others a flue connects with the main chimney. Some are brick-built, others stone. The ancient rights of commoners often included the collection of brushwood or ling for heating ovens. When the fuel had been burnt in them, the ashes were raked out, the dough placed inside and the door quickly closed.

Up to about 100 years ago, the kail pot was used for boiling and as an oven for

[1] In 1677 Christopher Norton of Temple Dowsker, Wensleydale, who had property in Bishopdale, gave as one reason for incurring debts 'the repair of several large Seate Houses'. [MS. in authors' possession.]

baking bread, pies and cakes, including the Christmas cake. A large, flat, cast-iron pan with a lid, it had three small feet, which, when it was stood on the hearth, allowed a draught for the fire to burn underneath it (*see page* 5). Red-hot peats were heaped on top of the lid.

In the eighteenth century with the introduction of the hob grate burning coal, the kitchen range consisted simply of blacksmith-made bars and grate fixed between two stone hobs. Over the fire, kettles and pans were suspended from the reckan-crook. Types of spits and jacks and later, large Dutch ovens, which incorporated a bottle jack to turn the joint, were used for roasting, mostly in larger houses only; for in general, meat and bacon were boiled. A big iron pot was almost always hanging over the fire. Oatcake had its own baking implements; for this together with porridge and broths was the basis of diet. Wooden and steel toasters and trivets were common.

Towards the end of the eighteenth century, by utilizing the hobs of the simple range, there developed the cast-iron oven and side boiler, supplied by foundries and fitted by ironmongers and blacksmiths, who ordered 'a set of fixtures' and made the central bars (the original range), the lid for the boiler and any detail, additional to the main parts. The oven, fitted with brass-looped handles, and the front of the boiler, were decorated with raised patterns, of which one representing the sun's rays became popular. The earliest were provided with small doors and compartments under both oven and boiler, so that separate fires might be lit directly under them as occasion demanded. In the next development the oven was heated from the main fire by a flue underneath and up the side of the oven farthest from the fire. Once heated, the old cast-iron ovens were 'hot for t' day', and although they were small, batch after batch of the loaves needed for the large families of the nineteenth century were baked in them (*see plates* 7, 9, 11).

The fittings of a kitchen, now an outhouse, at Low Haycote, Gawthrop, Dent, picture for us the 'house', that is the kitchen or workplace as opposed to the parlour—the room used for leisure. It has a range, bakstone alongside, large stone cheese press in a recess and a stone *slopstone* or sink (*see plate* 43). In upper Swaledale the house is still spoken of as the 'forehouse'.

An integral part of the early ranges was the *sooker-stone*, a large stone flag which filled in all the space above the oven and boiler, forming the flue. Its name and purpose derived from the canopy of the open hearth which drew or sucked up the smoke.

With the advent of the sooker, the flat steel bar called the reckan was fixed on to its face, and the crane pivoted from the top of the oven or boiler. Cranes of steel and sometimes of oak, were called *beaks* in Nidderdale. In sixteenth- and seventeenth-century wills, reckan-crooks were left as heirlooms, and in the last century it was customary for the Robinsons, blacksmiths of Redmire, Wensleydale, to make one to give to a newly-married couple. Although most of those in the dales are simple in design, they sometimes swivel in a variety of ways, and are rendered decorative by the keyhole-shaped openings in the bar in which the crooks are moved up and down. Hours were spent by the women polishing them until they shone 'like a mirror which you could see your face in'. Wright gives the delightful example of dialect from North Yorkshire: 'He's writin' reckin-creeaks.'

In the latter half of the nineteenth century, the hot-air oven, in which heat circulated in flues underneath and on both sides of the oven, began to replace the old small ovens. Above it were three knobs. The central one regulated the heat, whilst the other two worked scraper rods which when pushed and pulled in and out cleaned the soot off the flues at either side of the oven. This type of oven, with sheet-iron sides, heated up and cooled off quickly, and it was often added to the old range replacing the old cast-iron oven but leaving the water boiler intact.

Whereas the old ranges sometimes had on them the names of the foundry which made them, the later ones had the names of the ironmongers who fitted them such as Spence of Richmond, Iveson of Hawes, Manby of Skipton and Todd Bros. of Summerbridge, Nidderdale. Both Manby's and Todd's at one time ran foundries.

Complete ranges, their modernity proclaimed by the iron plates replacing the sooker, were themselves superseded by the Yorkists, Triplexes, and closed ranges such as Rayburns, and lastly by electric cookers. In the same way the old water boilers, from which all the hot water supply for the household had to be ladled out with a dipper, improved later by the addition of a tap, were done away with as hot water systems were installed in this century.

The hearthstone, pronounced 'asten', was formerly damped with milk to darken it and decorated with squirls and curlicues drawn on its border with a piece of light-coloured sandstone after each week's cleaning. People knew where to find suitable stone and picked a piece up in a gill when they were passing. It was customary to paint the jambs and lintel of the fireplace with tar or paint and sometimes to add flecks of different colours. The ashes fell into a deep pit covered with a grate, occasionally emptied.

To clean and polish the stone-flagged floors, which covered all the downstairs rooms, sand was sprinkled on them after washing—perhaps twice a week but

HEARTH FURNISHINGS

1 Reckan. 2 Crane, cottage, Main Street, Sedbergh. 3 Reckan and bar, Baldersdale. 4 Crane, Craven Arms, Appletreewick, Wharfedale. 5 Grate, Dent. 6 Trivet, Wensleydale. 7 Dutch oven. 8 Bottle jack. 9 Bellows. 10 Tinder box and striker. 11 Kail pot. 12 Bellows. 13 Bukker. 14 Toasting dog. 15 Cradle, Swaledale. 16 Dutch oven and spit.

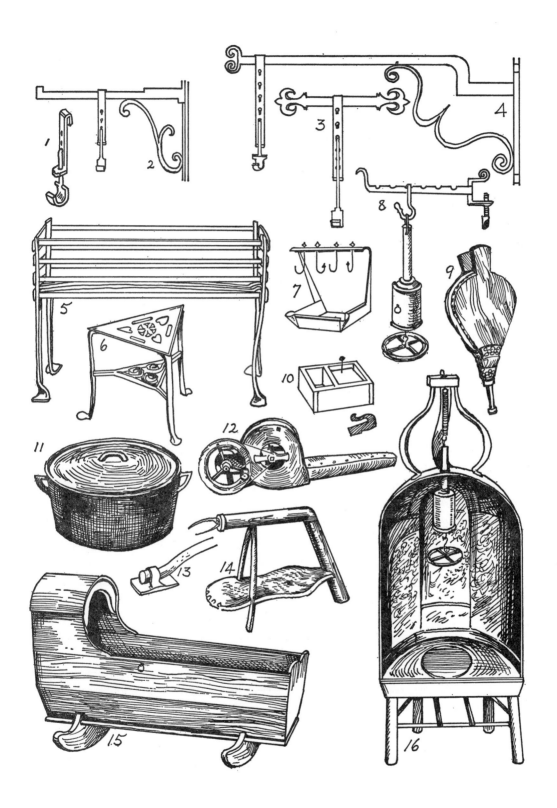

always on Fridays—then swept up the following day and rugs put down for Sunday. At times sand was fetched from the shores of tarns as was *lea* (scythe) sand, but usually pieces of soft sandstone were brayed fine with a *bukker* (flat iron hammer) on the *bink* (a stone slab on which milk pails were put to dry). No house was without its sand bucket and elderly people remember the penetrating squeak of clogs on the sanded floors.

A feature generally appearing directly above the fireplace was the beef loft, still to be seen occasionally but seldom complete with hooks, in Langstrothdale and in the dales round Sedbergh. When the flues began to be erected, upper floors were extended so that the space open to the rafters was lost. Into this a beef loft was often built. It was a box-like compartment, measuring about 8 ft. long by 4 ft. 6 ins. wide and 1 ft. 8 ins. high, open to the kitchen below and projecting its full height into the bedroom above. The space taken up in the bedroom was sometimes partitioned off to form a small room or cupboard, and when left unenclosed it appeared as a large box, which people remember using as a bed. On the underside of the beams which made the top of the loft, were fixed as many as twenty to thirty hooks. In this compartment, over the fire in the kitchen, joints of pickled beef or hams or sides of bacon were hung for winter use. It was too hot a place in which to leave hams and bacon for long and usually these were dried on a bacon flake, a rare object nowadays (*see plate* 44).

When cattle were brought indoors about Martinmas (11th November) the beef was prepared. Often one of the Scotch cattle was bought for the purpose at a May or July Fair and summered to give it a bit of flesh; or a beast was bought communally at a back-end fair, or a bull or cow from the farmer's herd was killed, cut up and dry salted in the *flesh* or *priming kit* (salting tub).

Dry salting appears to have been the early process. Mr J. Foster of Beckermonds has described how he remembers the method fifty or sixty years ago. One of their own cattle was usually killed, cut up and the ribs boned and rolled. (Flitches of beef appear in seventeenth-century wills.) From a large block of salt, a very little saltpetre, and water a brine was made by boiling in the set pot (fixed pan for boiling clothes in) until it was of the strength to float an egg. Then, when cold, the joints were immersed in it. The large thick legs were in for a month. They pickled all except what they could eat at the time. 'There was a lot on a beeast, and if ther' wasn't room for all i' t' beef loft, it was hung upstairs on hooks on t' joists. Meeast o' t' farms 'ud 'ev a beef loft.' The meat was always cooked by boiling a piece weighing about a stone, and at the same time some fat bacon was also boiled to go with it. Some state that if a stringy Scotch beast had been pickled, it was only poor stuff, and others recollect the bacon fat inches thick, but Mr Foster said that the beef was good to eat. 'It maks mi mouth watter to think on 't.' In the winter of 1895, when no cart came up the dale for fourteen weeks, they had plenty in hand at Beckermonds—flour, potatoes, salt meat and *clapbread* (oatcake).

In *A Memorial of Cowgill Chapel* (1868) Adam Sedgwick describes the furnishings of a *statesman's* (yeoman's) house in Dent. 'From one side of the fireplace ran a bench, with a strong and sometimes ornamentally carved back, called a *lang settle*. On the other side of the fireplace was the Patriarch's wooden and well-carved arm-chair; and near the chair was the sconce adorned with crockery. Not far off was commonly seen a well-carved cupboard, or cabinet, marked with some date that fell within a period of fifty years after the restoration of Charles II. One or two small tables, together with chairs and benches, gave seats to all the party assembled. . . .'

Nowadays, the typical furnishings of a yeoman's home sold over the centuries to dealers are nowhere to be found complete. In the Victorian era, fashion demanded different furniture, of a lighter colour, and in fact the old oak was sometimes painted. Where they still remain, the carved initials on the cupboards and *kists* (chests) seldom tally with the initials of the owners. At Low Hall, Garsdale, the old home of the Inmans, is a cupboard with the initials and date HLI 1654 coeval with the house; for the wall behind it is unplastered. Long settles, varying in size, and in deal, mahogany and oak, may still be seen, but seldom placed, as they once were, at right angles to the fireside. The sconce or *speer*, originating in the screen protecting the door from draughts or for privacy, remains at How, Lunedale, and at West New House, Bishopdale.

A rare feature is the cupboard bed, a survival of beds in living-rooms, usually the parlour. One, dating from the seventeenth century, formerly existed at Stone House, upper Swaledale, and another at Start House, Baldersdale. A third, sited under the stairs in the 'house' at West Nettlepot, Lunedale, had wooden lats, which supported a straw mattress topped by a feather bed. It was occupied by an elderly aunt quite recently. A fourth exists at Mickleton, in Teesdale. It is remembered that a cupboard bed in a cottage at Horton-in-Ribblesdale was known as the 'maternity bed'. On the other hand folding beds, which shut up into a piece of furniture resembling a wardrobe, were common. Kept in the living-rooms, they were useful for the accommodation of visitors.

Four-posters are remembered in upper Swaledale with a frill round the top and with check curtains which drew all the way round. One in Baldersdale still retains a pleated red alpaca canopy, with a fringe round the top, a bed-head and valances of the same material. The curtains gave privacy in bedrooms entered one from another, and witchstones—small pieces of limestone with a water-worn hole in them—hung on four-posters, warded off evil. The straw mattresses and feather beds were held up by ropes threaded through holes in the bedstocks. 'A curtained bed half-filled with musty mattresses was the usual form', said a writer in the *Settle Chronicle* (1854). The bed clothes often consisted of home-made quilts.

Grandfather clocks, the making of which was once a dales' craft, centred on Askrigg, Skipton, Settle and other places, are not mentioned by Professor Sedgwick, nor are so-called bible boxes or corner cupboards. Dating back to the seventeenth century, grandfather clocks became, as time went on and as the number of makers increased, an essential part of the furnishings of the farmhouse. It was customary and still is in some houses to keep the time shown half-an-hour forward.

Here and there a few interiors dating from the last century can be seen, centred on a big black kitchen range. Seventeenth-century oak panelling is rare; and the farmhouses with it are usually the halls. Especially in Dent, small cupboards with carved doors are let into the walls. Panelling of the next century (to be seen at Nappa Hall, Wensleydale) is mostly confined to town houses. The walls of old houses are occasionally adorned with plaster work and we have found remains of stencilling, with which around the middle of the last century it was fashionable to decorate walls. Some have stylized designs, others patterns of birds, others a simple formal design of blue diamonds and dots. Everywhere in the old days, walls were covered with yellow ochre or blue or white limewash. The best bedroom was generally the first room to be papered.

Lighting developed from the now rarely found double oil lamp, the Scottish *crusie*, to rushlights and candles, which were made from the pith of *seaves* (rushes) dipped in tallow. Candles, bought from small candle factories, such as Candle Willie's at Burtersett, Wensleydale, were hung by the wicks, which ran through them all, from the kitchen beams and cut off as required. Candle boxes and snuffers are some of the most common of bygones; and the unpleasant smell of rancid tallow, when the candle was snuffed, is still remembered. Paraffin oil lamps, usually only one to a house, are still found, but very rarely. People used to sit by the firelight and seldom possessed *shades* (thin blinds or curtains); they were up and went to bed, early.

The dairy, complete with stone shelves, and occasionally called the buttery, is on the north side, not usually in a cellar, which is reserved for large or manor houses. Combined with the kitchen, the scene of butter and cheese making, it contained dairy utensils, food and crockery and baking equipment, as it still does. Whitened twice a year, the degree of whiteness is a matter of pride to the farmer's wife. Near to the outer door grew an elderbush to keep off flies, and on which butter muslin and cloths might be dried. Similarly making use of what was available, a branch of a gooseberry bush, a goose's wing or a bunch of ling, weighted

SWALEDALE QUILTING PATTERNS

*1 Chain border. 2 Fern. 3 Heart. 4 Central pattern star and rose. 5 Feather. 6 Bellows and star.
7 Fern. 8 Prince of Wales feather. 9 Prince of Wales feather. 10 Plant pot of tulips. 11 Diamond
pattern for the background. 12 Fan used for corners. 13 Border made with a cup.*

with a stone and let down from the top, served as a brush for sweeping the chimney.

Now and again we have come across a large old mangle, sometimes utilized as a table in a back kitchen, which was formerly used for mangling sheets only. Iron wash-boilers were hung over the fire from the reckans, while wooden tubs, Peggy tubs and dolly-sticks and other types of old mangles and set boilers have gone comparatively recently.

Outside the house the privy, *necessary* or *nessy* as it was called within recollection, was usually a small separate building. Some, such as a well-built one at Woodhouse Manor, now used as a garden tool-shed, date from the seventeenth century. One, pulled out comparatively recently in upper Wensleydale, had three holes, graded in size from large to small, in the seat. Another in the bedroom of a derelict farm-house in Swaledale emulated the castle necessary with a shute on to an outside wall. It certainly obviated the use of the lantern for the journey down the garden path at night.

In this century, farmhouse kitchens are still comfortable places; but perhaps the 'house' was at its best fifty years ago when large families were brought up, when little was bought, when hams and sides of bacon, pickled beef, herbs and charms such as strings of blown eggs or witchstones were hung up to ward off evil spirits, when home-made butter and cheese, bread and cheese-cakes filled the dairy, and havercake found a place on the ceiling-boards together with caps, hats and boots. But what work it represented!

DAIRY WORK

BECAUSE of the pastoral character of the dales the importance of cattle, either for rearing for beef or for cows giving milk to make into butter and cheese, has been and is prominent, and certain dales, notably Nidderdale, Wensleydale and Dent, excelled in dairy produce. It was said of Pateley Bridge, Nidderdale, in *General View of Agriculture of the West Riding* (1794): 'Much butter is also salted here, and sent to York for the London market. One person alone exports from 700 to 800 firkins annually of 56 lb. per firkin—the price for which it is contracted at, is 38s. per firkin. A cow in the dale produces about 3 firkins during the season; but upon the higher grounds only 2 firkins.' Of Dent it was stated, 'A great number of milk cows are kept, and large quantities of butter and cheese produced'; and within recollection the making of butter boxes, constructed for the carriage of butter, was a speciality of the dale. Wensleydale, giving its name to an English cheese, has a continuous record of cheese making for eight centuries.

In 1150, cheese, at that time made from ewes' milk, is mentioned in an inventory of the stock and assets of Fors Abbey (the precursor of Jervaulx), Wensleydale. Harrison[1] writing in Elizabethan times reported: 'Some housewives can and doe ad dailie a lesse proportion of ewes milke unto [the milk of] so manie kine, whereby their cheese doth the longer abide moist, and eateth more brickle and mellow than other wise it would.' Indeed we have a record of the milking of both ewes and cows at Blean and Stalling Busk, near Semerwater (and the collection of butter and cheese by a factor) at about the same time as Harrison was writing.[2] But as stock improved and increased, cheese ceased to be made from ewes' milk.

When cheese fairs were inaugurated at Leyburn, Wensleydale, in the 1840's, the name Wensleydale for the particular mild cheese of this and the surrounding dales appears to have been adopted. It may have been made slightly differently, and *prezzur* (the liquid obtained by boiling keslops, the dried stomach of a calf) was used as the curding agent. W. Livesey, quoted in *Dairy Farming* by J. P. Sheldon, writes of a changeover from an old method to a new during the latter half of the

---

[1] *Description of England in Shakespeare's Youth*, Book iii, chap. i, p. 8.
[2] P.R.O. E 178/2627. Exch. Spec. Commissions, York 21 & 22 Eliz. (1579/80.)

nineteenth century. But we have not had this confirmed by oral tradition. Following the opening of the Department of Agriculture at Leeds University in 1890 and the eventual formation of an advisory service with instructors, the methods of cheese making (and butter making) were improved and stabilized.

In the 1870's, Livesey said that the biggest cheese made in Wensleydale weighed twenty pounds and the majority, ten to fifteen pounds, with some as small as four or five pounds. Generally the dairy consisted of from seven to ten cows, with a few running up to sixteen or twenty. Cheeses were made from a dairy of five, four or even three cows, and at a farm where seven cows were kept, they made two a day.

In the past there were problems at all stages of milk, butter and cheese production as well as marketing. The cows were milked out of doors in summer and indoors in low dark cowsheds in winter. The milk was carried from field or cowshed to the farmhouse in a *budget*, more often called a *backcan*, a specially shaped tin can to fit the back (*see plate* 98), by both men and women. *Headcans*, with a slight hollow for the head, were used for the same purpose. Whether or not the budgets here were ever made of wood or leather, we may only surmise.[1] But the use of budgets or backcans, then unique in the United Kingdom, ceased in general soon after the Second World War.

Backcans varied in size from small ones for children to ones holding four to eight gallons. They were carried like a rucksack by leather or webbing straps over both shoulders. The backcan ideally was transported full, otherwise, although it had an inner lid, the milk swilled about. It is remembered in many parts how the children went up to the pastures whilst the men and women were milking and were given a drink of milk from the backcan lid.

In Wensleydale, donkeys were formerly much used for carrying milk—the last donkey, long since pensioned off, died at Castle Bolton in 1967—and in Swaledale small ponies were used. A milk crate or *hebble* was slung over the animal's back on a sack, and backcans, equally full, placed on each side (*see plate* 99). At Stalling Busk there are ten fields of about an acre each known as the 'Donkey Folds' and the track to the old cow-pasture is the 'Donkey Trod'.

Besides the milking out of doors, proper care and cleanliness were not always observed in the dairy work, and handling at markets left much to be desired. The best produce was excellent, but the worst was poor. Much butter, rancid and

---

[1] In *Adamnani Vita S. Columbae*, A. O. and M. O. Andersen, Edinburgh (1961), Columba is described as carrying a wooden milk pail on his back. It had a bar through two holes to hold down the lid. In *History of Technology*, vol. II, The Mediterranean Civilizations and the Middle Ages, 'Vehicles and Harness' shows a water-seller with ass and leather budget from the Luttrell Psalter *c.* 1338.

uneatable, went for salving sheep, and old or skim milk cheese made in Wensleydale, where it was called old peg cheese, or Whangby cheese, made in Wharfedale,
was hard and tough—tough enough to make *whangs* (thongs) of it.[1]

On a cheese farm it was usually arranged for the cows to calve in the spring, and
from May to October, whilst they were grazing on the pastures, cheese was made.
Some farms continued to make a little cheese in winter, but most with any milk to
spare, turned over then to butter making. The farmer's wife, with the help of a
daughter, controlled the cheese making whilst another daughter, if there was no
dairy maid, concentrated on the butter-making. Approximately one gallon of milk
makes one to one and a half pounds of cheese, but the longer a cheese is kept, the
more it dries and loses weight. The ones manufactured at the beginning and end
of the season were the well-known flat shape, whilst those destined to go 'blue'
and be kept for Christmas, made from June to September, were usually Stilton-
shaped. The famous 'blue' Wensleydale resulted from the mould in the cheese
room and often they were pricked to hasten the desired effect.

When the cows were first put out to grass, the resulting cheese made from their
milk was known as 'grass cheese'; 'pasture cheese' was the type to go 'blue'; 'fog
cheese' was made when the cows were eating the fog—the aftermath of the hay—
and 'hay cheese', made in winter, was a variety which inclined to be a little tough
and hard.

Every farm had its dairy utensils, formerly mostly of wood or pot and latterly
tinned plate or aluminium. We should like to have seen those belonging to
Galfryd Calvert of Burton in 'Busshopdaill' who, when he died in 1575, had three
'litle wod cheisfatts' one 'milk syle' (sieve) one 'mylke kytt' and three 'litle olde
wod bowells' all worth 1d. or 2d. each.[2] Two stones of cheese were bought for
his funeral. In lists of sales the cheese kettle, either in brass or copper and later
made of tin, was by far the most valuable item of dairy equipment. Besides this
were the *brig* for *t'sile* (bridge for the sieve), a breaker, grinder, *chesfords* (cheese
vats) and presses (*see drawings on page* 15 *and plates* 21–5). Usually made by the local
cooper, chesfords were of oak and the *sinkers* (lids) of elm. Wooden cheese
presses are extremely rare. Stone presses, seen rather more frequently, required
either an outhouse or an alcove to house them, and were superseded by iron
presses.

Many people still remember cheese making.[3] They recollect the 'herby' land of
limestone pasture as a first-class feed for stock producing milk for cheese. They

[1] Carr's *Dialect of Craven.*
[2] *Wills and Inventories in the Archdeaconry of Richmond*, Surtees Society, vol. XXVI.
[3] For a recipe see *Practical Cheesemaking* by C. W. Walker-Tisdale and Walter E. Woodnutt (1917),
and *The Yorkshire Dales* by Marie Hartley and Joan Ingilby (1956), p. 312.

say that heifers give better milk than old cows, although some cows keep up the quality all their lives, and that milk from a cow ready to be served makes cheese bitter. In the same way, thinking of butter making, they fondly remember a cow that was a good 'creamer'; others with less pleasure recall a 'slow-turning churner', that is, a cow whose cream, if put amongst the rest, delays the churning.

As well as the actual making, which lasted on and off all day, each farm had a cheese room where the cheeses were stored on *traves* (shelves supported on stands). Cheese flakes or 'hangers to laye cheese on' existed at West Applegarth, Swaledale, in 1564.[1] Here, besides turning the cheese at first twice a day and later once, the cheese maker was constantly wiping down the shelves. Cheese runs more if a fine spell of weather is imminent, and the cheerful news that 'cheeses is runnin', we'll get on wi' t' hay' was part of the lore of Hill Top Farm, upper Swaledale.

Some towards the end, carried on cheese-making in a big way with large, zinc-lined cheese troughs running on wheels and heated with hot water in an outer jacket. Such a large cheese farm was Nether Hesleden, Littondale, where seventeen or eighteen cows were milked in summer and two or three, eight- to ten-pound cheeses made per day, with two or three cheese presses regularly in use and cheese sent to London for Christmas. Mrs W. Birkett, West Park, Cotherstone, made cheese, which she preferred to call Cotherstone rather than Wensleydale, long after most people had stopped, and in 1938 was sending cards to her customers all over England offering cheese at 1s. 3d. per pound for delivery in October or at 1s. 6d. per pound for delivery in November or December. At North Gill Farm, Lartington, Teesdale, four ten-pound cheeses were made daily. Forty years ago the Guys of Hill Top, upper Swaledale, milking fourteen cows, made three or four cheeses a day, and used the two large stone cheese presses which still remain there outside in an alcove. For many years at the turn of the century Mr J. R. Guy, starting at 3.30 a.m. and taking twenty to thirty cheeses, journeyed fortnightly to 'stand' Barnard Castle market where cheese was in demand for the miners of County Durham,[2] just as at present Wensleydale cheese is popular with the miners of South Yorkshire.

The sale at markets and fairs or to factors was the means of marketing both cheese and butter. Latterly Yarm Fair, held in October, provided the main outlet for cheese, much of which had been constantly turned and had lost weight all

[1] *Wills and Inventories in the Archdeaconry of Richmond*, Surtees Society, vol. XXVI.
[2] Told us by Mrs J. Chapman, *b*. Hill Top, Swaledale.

CHEESE-MAKING UTENSILS

1 Yoke. 2 Milking pail. 3 Sieve (sile). 4 Backcan. 5 Bridge (brig for the sile). 6 Tin cheese kettle. 7 Breaker. 8 Copper cheese kettle. 9 Grinder. 10 Cheese vats (chesfords) and sinker (lid).

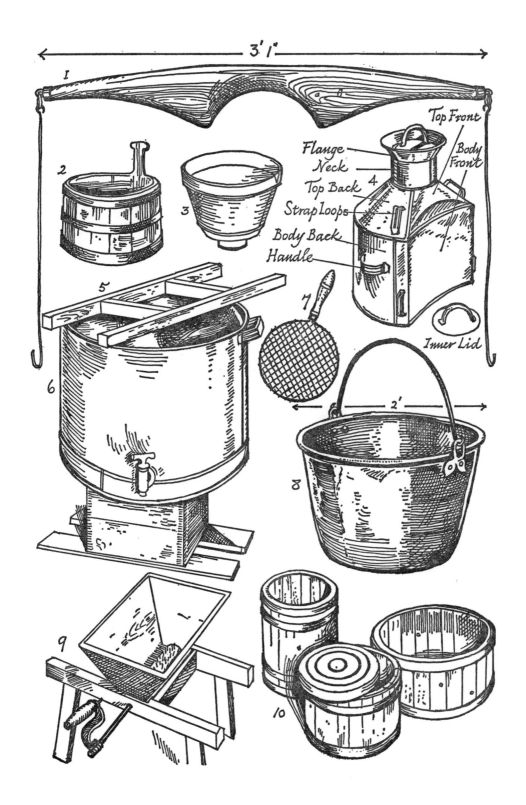

3' 1"

1

2

3

Flange
Neck
Top Back
Strap Loops
Body Back
Handle

Top Front
Body
Front

4

Inner Lid

5

7

6

2'

8

9

10

summer. About 1878 at Hawes, in the spring, when cheese makers for a time made butter, as much as 7,000 lbs. of butter might be sold in a single market day and 3,000 lbs. was usual.[1] Factors often represented grocers who sold groceries in exchange for dairy products—a system which encouraged the sale of inferior goods as the grocer did not wish to lose customers.

The last cheese factor in upper Wensleydale, Mr R. Hugill, started in 1921 with 7s. 6d. in his pocket. He borrowed £30 and hired a horse and flat cart one day a week, for which he was charged 3s. and had to deliver a load of meal. At the end of the first year he bought himself a bicycle. Travelling round the farms he graded and bought cheese and sold it to local shops. He remembers that once as he entered a cheese room the shelf broke, bringing the cheeses toppling down. He recollects too, after walking a long distance across a moor to an outside farm, that he found a woman making cheeses in 1-lb. jam jars. When she couldn't get them out she broke the jars. He bought a hundred at 4d. per pound and sold them the same day, fifty at Hawes and the rest at his home. 'They went like sweets.'

As for the butter, similar marketing conditions prevailed. Factors, packing it into butter boxes, travelled the dales. In upper Swaledale a hundred years ago, an old Scotsman, wearing a plaid and a 'Scotch hat', used to come from Bradford to buy it. Fifty years ago in Dent, the factor, known as the 'butter gatherer', gave small boys 1d. for knocking down *ramps* (garlic), which growing freely in some parts spoilt the taste of the butter. In Sedbergh some people walked to Kendal, eleven miles, to obtain 1d. per pound more. When we questioned the cost of this in footwear, we were assured that they mended their own boots. The following letter, dated 22nd January 1853, refers to Muker, Swaledale. 'Sir. We Shall be up/ on Monday for the Butter/ Pleas Let the Other/ Dairy Maids Know/ Your Kindness/ Will much Oblidge/ John Jackson.'

Like cheese making, butter making has its own implements: churns ranging in size from small to large, wooden bowls for standing the milk in and for *clashing* in the making process, lead bowls used for separating, *weigh bogeys* (scales), a butter plate, a slate, prints, and towards the end Scotch hands (flat wooden patters).

Butter making occupied much of the space in the dairy, for before separators were invented, the milk was stood in wooden, crockery or lead bowls for the cream to rise. The heavy, shallow, oblong lead-lined bowls rested on stone dairy shelves, which often had a hole bored in them, so that the skim milk could be run off through the hole in the centre of the lead bowl and drop down into a pail under the dairy shelf, leaving the cream behind sticking to the lead whence it was scraped off often with a horn or whalebone scraper into a cream pot.

The use of the early plunge churn, usually called a stand churn in the dales, is still

[1] *Routh's Guide to Wensleydale* (1878).

1. *West New House, Bishopdale, dated 1635. A good example of a farmhouse with a central chimney stack and the barn and buildings under one roof.*

2. *Old Cotes, Littondale, dated 1650, as it appeared before alterations when the barn was pulled down in 1914. The spiral staircase is seen on the left of the porch.*

FARMHOUSES

3. *Miss H. Reeves in the kitchen at Agglethorpe Hall, Coverdale. A range with a hot-air oven fills in the seventeenth-century arch.*

4. *Sconce, How Farm, Lunedale.*

FARMHOUSE
KITCHENS

5. *Fireplace at Longridge, Bishopdale, a house dated 1653; the arch is 13 ft 4 in. wide and the inglenook 4 ft deep with a brick oven on the right side, and a smaller arch on the right.*

6. *Seventeenth-century fireplace at Riverside, Coverdale. The arch is one of a small group of similar arches, found in Coverdale and Nidderdale. It consists of three stones, the keystone and two large stones at each side of it, chiselled to represent smaller stones. There is a brick oven on the left of the recess.*

17th-CENTURY FIREPLACES

19th-CENTURY FIREPLACE & SETTLE

7. *A fireplace at Low Hall, Garsdale, with ogee-shaped sooker stone. It is marked 'Low Moor', probably cast by Hird, Dawson, Hardy and Field, iron-founders of Bradford, who flourished in the 1830s. The kail pot, in use in the last century, hangs from reckan and crane.*

8. *Long settle, formerly at the side of the fireplace, at Agglethorpe Hall. The rail held a curtain which was drawn across at night.*

19th-CENTURY FIREPLACES

9. *The fireplace at the Cottage, Skellgill, Wensleydale, marked 'Ingram Founder Ripon' with sun's rays decoration and sooker stone. It dates from about 1820.*

10. *A fireplace at Blayshaw, Nidderdale, marked 'Todd Bros. Summerbridge'—late but complete example. The steel bar is attached to a tin sooker. A bakstone once stood alongside.*

COTTAGE

11. *Mr J. T. Alderson, Pitcher House, Baldersdale, and fireplace showing painted surround usual fifty years ago. The oven on the left is older than the boiler on the right. Note crane and sooker stone; also on right of fireplace, spoon-rack, pincushion, letter rack, drenching horn and horse bit.*

FARMHOUSE

12. *Mr J. B. Raine and Mrs J. A. Allison, West Nettle-pot, Lunedale; fireplace, with crane and hot-air oven, painted all over.*

KITCHENS

13. *Mrs Cooper Metcalfe, Starling Castle, upper Swaledale. Range with hot-air oven and on the right boiler with sun's rays decoration; sooker into which is fixed a bar from which the reckans hang. The tin sheet with two knobs was a common addition to help the draught.*

KITCHEN

14. *Cupboard bed at West Nettlepot. This utilizes a space under the stairs, allowing room for a bed 6 ft 6 in. long and 4 ft 4 in. wide.*

15. *Stuffed, small green parrot with a red cherry in its beak. The inscription on the back of the case reads: 'This parrot came by itself to Nettle Pot March 7 1834 and died July 14 1850.'*

16. *Court cupboard with the initials and date HLI 1654, Low Hall, Garsdale, the old home of the Inmans.*

17. *Pewter and furniture belonging to the Garths, Haverdale House, Swaledale.*

18. *Late seventeenth-century grandfather clock made by John Ogden in Wensleydale. It has 'John Ogden Bowbrighall' inscribed on the dial, the initials I A C carved on the door of the case and an early verge-type escapement with a short bob-weight pendulum. Owned by Mr and Mrs Dyson, Altofts.*

FURNITURE

remembered. Held loosely by one hand and twisted by the other, the staff was plunged up and down. The worker best kept an even pace, and did not pump up to the lid or splashing would result. If, when the butter was coming, it was not held down firmly, the whole churn tended to lift with the upward pull.

Barrel churns, invented in the eighteenth century, eventually replaced the stand churns, as did tub and fly churns. These contained dashers or flies inside, which were turned by a handle. The barrel churns often had two handles, occasionally wound by men rather than women. Lastly, came the end-over-end churn, invented it is thought about 1880 by the present Mr D. G. Waide's great grandfather, W. Waide, the founder of the firm of that name in Leeds in 1845. Called the Victoria Churn, and dependent not on dashers but on the end-over-end action, this won innumerable prizes and medals at agricultural shows and was copied by other makers. It ranged in size in Waide's list of 1891 from a churn holding a quart to two gallons of cream, making half a pound to six pounds of butter, costing £2 10s., to one holding six to thirty-five gallons of cream making ten to 105 lb. of butter, costing £8 10s. Waide's of Leeds only ceased to make churns in November 1966, and they, Hopperton's of Darlington and York, and Richardson's of Kendal supplied much of the dairy equipment used in the dales' farmhouse dairies.

Temperatures, which vary with that of the dairy, are vital in butter-making; and stories of the difficulties experienced in churning are legion. In the dales, cold weather often caused the trouble. When the butter would not come at all, it was said that it had gone to sleep. A cure was to put a little warm milk or water (or in summer, cold water) in the churn. Mr J. Swales, born 1874, of Low Wood, near Pateley Bridge, remembers a family story of his grandfather, born about 1812, going to Ripon to see the wise woman because the butter would not come, and how she gave him some horseshoe nails in a bottle to be buried in the churchyard. Similarly, Margaret Little of Lowlands, Askrigg, Wensleydale, used to put a poker across the top of her stand churn to keep witches away. Another old man in Nidderdale held the record for churning—seven o'clock in the morning until seven o'clock at night—and even then he didn't get any butter.

Following churning, the butter was clashed by hand in the butter bowl to remove the butter milk, a method superseded by the invention of butter-workers in the latter half of the last century (*see drawings on page* 19 *and plates* 29–30). The butter-worker obviated touching the butter. Next, the expert maker, requiring to separate the butter into pounds, usually judged the weight 'dead on'. Often if they were not to be collected for a day or two they put $\frac{1}{2}$d. or 1d. on the weight to ensure that the pounds did not 'dry out light'.

Lastly, the butter was shaped for printing, either into round cones for printing with round prints, or rolls for marking with a roller, or in later times made into the oblong shape of today and adorned with Scotch hands at lightning speed with diamonds, squares, leaves and so on. Although formerly each farm had its prints or markers by which it was known, such as the Greenbanks, formerly of Dry Beck, Ribblesdale, who had one depicting daisies and leaves, latterly the designs—a rose, shamrock, thistle, cow, a sheaf of corn and others—were used more indiscriminately. At Nether Lodge, upper Ribblesdale, the Morphets made 'riggin' pounds, like a small oblong house with a rigging, which, when one layer was placed one way up and the next the other, compactly filled a butter box. In other cases, as in Coverdale, butter was sold in 24-oz. rolls.

Like the cheese makers, the butter makers remember the difficulties, the hard work and the good and bad times. Again applying to both butter and cheese making, the farmer's wife, daughter or hired help, only excelled if she had a light hand. Mrs J. Postlethwaite, formerly of Riddings, Howgill, near Sedbergh, remembers making 100 lb. every week with an end-over-end churn, and that when it became hard work, she knew she had nearly done. Mrs T. J. Middleton, Gawthrop, Dent, used to make 90 lb. at home and 80 lb. at her brother's, totalling 170 lb. in a day.

In the 1930's the price of farmhouse butter and cheese reached bedrock. One week in 1939, Mr H. Moon of The Arches, Bolton Abbey, took sixty pounds of butter to Skipton market, and sold only ten pounds at 1s. per pound. Elsewhere it dropped to 6d., a price at which Wensleydale cheese was sold. This was less than the 8d. to 11d. which had obtained in the 1840's.[1] Small wonder that the cheese and butter makers of the dales went over to selling liquid milk. Nor were there any longer the large families to help with the work.

Since the 1890's milk has been sent away from Wensleydale by train and cheese factories at Hawes, Coverham and elsewhere have been started. The formation of the Milk Marketing Board in 1933 consolidated the trend. Up to October 1939 there were 433 cheese-makers in Wensleydale, Swaledale and Teesdale, including some outlying farms elsewhere.[2] In 1957 the last registered maker went out of production.[3] Almost all cheese and butter is now manufactured in factories, and if the best quality has gone, good factory-made cheese is uniform in quality and the drudgery of dairy work has left the farmhouse.

[1] *Wensleydale Advertiser* 2nd January 1844 (10d.), 24th December 1844 (11d.), 8th July 1845 (8d.).
[2] Mr R. Hugill, Askrigg, Wensleydale.
[3] The Milk Marketing Board.

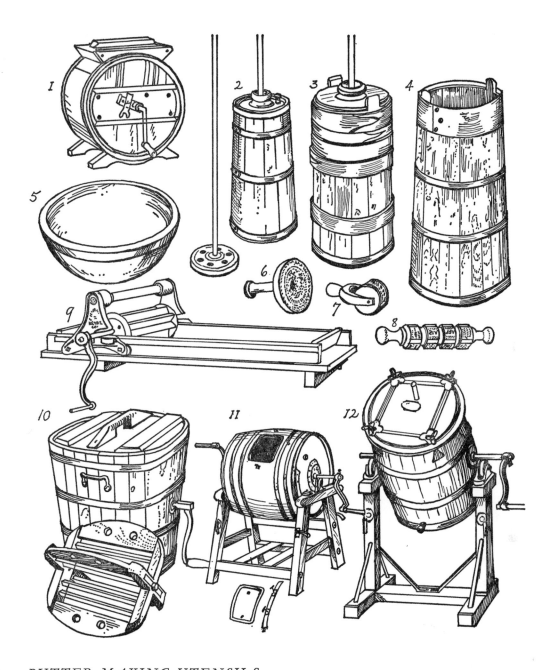

BUTTER-MAKING UTENSILS

1 Table churn. 2 Stand churn, hooped with iron girths, and plunger. 3 Stand churn, hooped with ash bands. 4 Large stand churn. 5 Butter bowl. 6 Butter print. 7 Roller marker. 8 Roller marker. 9 Butter-worker. 10 Tub churn and dasher. 11 Waide's barrel churn as pictured in a catalogue of 1891. 12 Waide's Victoria or end-over-end churn as pictured in the same catalogue.

OATCAKE

BECAUSE oats were a feasible crop in regions of high altitude and a cold wet climate, oatmeal was formerly the basis of diet in the hill country of Britain. Whereas the north-west Yorkshire Dales are now mostly under grass, arable fields existed there in the Middle Ages. Cultivation terraces are visible alongside many villages in many dales, and references to the growing of oats, barley and wheat appear in tithe disputes.

From the earliest times every village and hamlet had one or more water corn mills at which corn grown locally was ground. In time as arable land was enclosed and turned into meadow—a widespread trend in the reign of Elizabeth I—and as the population increased, more and more corn was imported. Mill account books record that in the eighteenth century households bought oatmeal weekly or monthly often alternately with wheatmeal in proportion as their means allowed.

In his *State of the Poor* (1797) Eden says of Skipton: 'Oatmeal is made into bread, and, sometimes into hasty-pudding: this wholesome and nutritious diet is, however, falling into disuse.' Whitaker writing of Linton, Wharfedale, in the eighteenth century in his *History of Craven* (1805) says: 'They all grew oats, which formed the principal article of their subsistence: the kiln in which the grain was parched previous to its being ground belonged to the township at large, and when in use was a sort of village coffee-house where the politics of the place and the day were discussed. Of oatmeal their bread was invariably made, and most of their puddings; and this, mixed with milk, or water when milk was scarce, supplied them with breakfast and supper.'

In *North Country Words* (1674) Ray gives several kinds of oatcake, of which *tharve-cakes*, clapbread and *riddlecakes* or *riddlebread* were still being made in the early years of the twentieth century when the baking of oatcake ceased or was thenceforward dying out. So, in searching for them today we are reaching back to age-old traditional types and methods of baking.

The varieties fall into two groups: the first was made from a dough or stiff paste rolled out with a rolling pin and baked either on a built-in bakstone or a girdle, always called a bakstone. This was *havercake*, haverbread or clapbread and *clapcake*, of which the latter took its name from the old method now forgotten of clapping it out with the hand on a concave board.[1] The second was made from a batter, often called a dough, containing leaven either *barm* (yeast) or less traditionally bi-carbonate of soda, and usually baked by throwing or pouring on to a built-in bakstone. This type was called either riddlebread or oatcake.

The following table shows where, within living memory, the different types were baked. It will be noted that the main regional difference is between the havercake of the dales of the North Riding and the other types made in the dales of the West Riding, and that the names with the prefix *haver*, from Old Norse *hafri* meaning oats, occur in areas of strong Norse colonization.

NAME	METHOD	DALE
Havercake	Made by rolling out a stiff paste of oatmeal, water and salt and baking on a girdle, a round portable iron bakstone.	The North Riding Dales of Wensleydale, Swaledale and sometimes in Teesdale.
Haverbread	Rolled out and baked on a built-in bakstone.	Round Sedbergh, Cautley, Howgill and Dent.
Riddlebread	Riddlebread made from a batter poured on a built-in bakstone.	Ribblesdale, round Ingle-borough, Bentham and in Bowland.
Clapbread	Clapbread rolled out and baked on the same type of bakstone.	
Oatcake	Made from a batter and thrown or poured on a bakstone.	Wharfedale and Malhamdale.
Havercake Haverbread Clapbread	Different names for the same type of oatbread made by rolling out and either baked on a girdle-type or built-in bakstone.	Langstrothdale and Dent, where several types overlap.
Tharve cake Short haver Watticake Oatcake	Tharve cake, a thick loaf made of whole meal baked on a girdle. Built-in bakstones existed but the methods are almost forgotten.	Nidderdale.

Originally bakstones were portable flat oval stones, common in the industrial West Riding but not seen or recollected in the Yorkshire Dales. However, Bak-stone Gills in several dales point to where suitable stone was once quarried. Lucas in *Studies in Nidderdale* (*c.* 1870) describes it as 'a very fine soft micaceous flaggy sandstone which stood the heat as well as a fire-brick', and he goes on to say that it made sweeter oatcake than did iron bakstones. One large fixed stone bakstone (a slab of smooth slate one and a half inches thick) but without the firebox remains

---

[1] *The Journeys of Celia Fiennes* (*1698*) Cresset Press (1947), pp. 193–4. (Description of clapbread made at Kendal.)

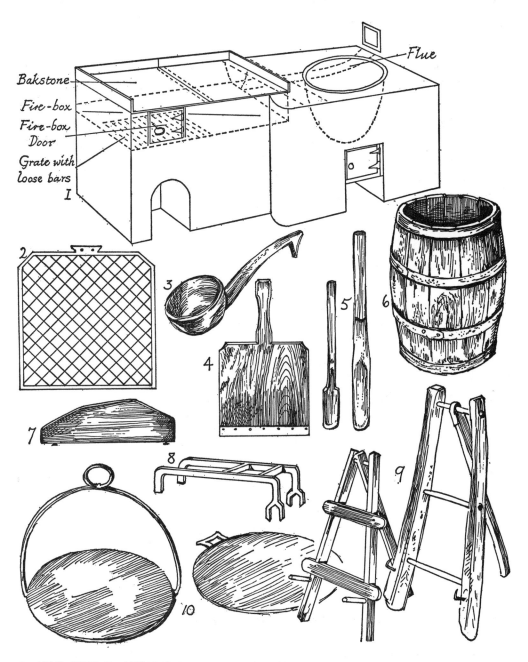

Bakstone

Fire-box

Fire-box
Door

Grate with
loose bars

Flue

1

2

3

4

5

6

7

8

9

10

OATCAKE BAKING IMPLEMENTS

*1 Bakstone and set pot formerly at Ruecrofts, Howgill, near Sedbergh. 2 Riddleboard. 3 Ladle.
4 Spittle. 5 Thibles. 6 Kneading tub. 7 Scraper. 8 Crow, for supporting the round iron bakstone.
9 Cake stools. 10 Iron bakstones. 3, 4, 5, 6 and 7 were used by the Redmaynes at South House, Selside,
upper Ribblesdale.*

at Knight Farm, Little Stainforth, Ribblesdale, and others are remembered at Bunker's Hill, Burnsall, Wharfedale, and at Old Cotes, Littondale.

Fixed or built-in bakstones had been invented by the beginning of the nineteenth century, for Walker depicts one in *The Costume of Yorkshire* (1814). This appears to be stone, but cast-iron plates had come into use by 1828 as Carr states in *Dialect of Craven*. Although it cannot be said that every farm had a bakstone, a great many had. We have actually seen fourteen. Sited next to the kitchen fireplace or in an outhouse sharing the flue with a set pot, most have been destroyed over the years.

Those in upper Ribblesdale, Malhamdale, Wharfedale and round Bentham and Bowland have iron plates measuring three feet by one foot six inches, whilst those round Sedbergh measure four feet by two feet, and, mostly in two plates, two feet by two feet, they have flanges on three sides (*see diagram on page* 23). Often the front of the bakstone is a single thick flag with holes cut out for the stoke-hole door and the ash pit. In the dales of the North Riding they were rare and are not remembered. One of the Sedbergh type remains at a cottage at Riggs House, Hawes, upper Wensleydale. In the large firebox underneath the whole of the plate turf, bracken, ling, gorse, broom, oat hulls, coal, sticks or wood shavings were burnt—anything in fact which was to hand to make a hot easily controlled fire. The stoke-hole door had a projecting handle designed for the insertion of a poker to open the door.

In the whole of the West Riding from Wharfedale to Bowland, also including the industrial districts, the thrown type of oatcake was made. (It was called oatcake in all the dales which concern us, except upper Ribblesdale and round Ingleborough where it was known as riddlebread.) Up to about 1850 oatcake was made by throwing the batter on to the bakstone, but gradually after that the method changed to pouring. At the North Ribblesdale Agricultural Show prizes were given annually for the best basket of oatcakes containing not less than six cakes, and in 1855, an extra class was introduced for six cakes 'made on the new system'. This eventually superseded the old method all over the dales where thrown oatcake had been made. Oral tradition also points to the changeover taking place about 100 years ago; and here and there *riddleboards*, unnecessary in the new system, are to be found.

The old system is described by Frederic Montagu in *Gleanings in Craven* (1838). 'The baker sprinkles oatmeal on the *backboard*, then pours on a ladleful of batter, rotates the board and transfers it [the batter] to a piece of linen or paper resting on the *spittle*. With this the batter is thrown on to a bakstone and the linen taken up.' Mrs J. Beckwith, born 1873, remembers when she was a girl using a round piece of brown paper for throwing the batter on to a girdle at New Houses, upper Nidderdale.

The implements were a backboard or riddleboard, a wooden ladle, spittle and tub for mixing (*see drawings on page* 23). Formerly the batter, often containing butter-milk, was mixed in a small wooden tub, which was not cleaned, so that the particles on the sides acted as a fermenting agent for the next baking. The quantity of buttermilk, which imparted a sour flavour, was a matter of choice. Some liked the product pale in colour, others brown. It may be noted that most commercial bakers of oatcake relied on the throwing action for which the bakstone was fitted with a special roller contrivance. (*See Gwerin*, vol. III, no. 2, 1960, 'Oatbread of Northern England' by Frank Atkinson.)

A further kitchen fixture necessary for the drying of the thrown oatcake was the flake (pronounced 'fleeak'), of which many examples, used for drying clothes, are still to be seen round Barden and Bolton Abbey. Those in Wharfedale had wooden lats and those in upper Ribblesdale had strings, over two of which the riddlebread was laid. The bread flake at Ling House, Threshfield, Wharfedale, measures ten feet six inches by four feet six inches, and has twenty-three cross bars.

In November 1965 Miss E. Carr, who had only recently ceased to make riddle-bread regularly, demonstrated the new system for us at a farmhouse near Bentham (*see plates* 34–9). The batter was prepared the same day by pouring a pint and a half of blue milk (in default of buttermilk) into an enamel pail, adding about three quarts of hot water to bring it to blood heat, then about six pounds of sieved oatmeal and one ounce of yeast with in addition a little bi-carbonate of soda. It was well stirred by hand and left for an hour near the fire to rise. (People often speak of wrapping an old coat round the pail at this stage.) A little more meal and water were then added to make a thick pouring consistency. A ladleful of batter, first trans-ferred into the basin, was poured on the bakstone and the scraper run over it to spread and control the size and thickness of the cake. Great pride in the shape and size of cake was shown. Very thin and soft after baking, it is rough on one side and smooth on the other. As the steam and roasting smell rose and as one by one the cakes were laid on a white cloth, we felt we were sharing in an age-old ritual. Butter was brought in and we were offered a 'buttercake'. When finally hung across the strings of the flake, they looked, as has been said before, exactly like washleather. While the cakes are soft, some people like to spread treacle on them; when they are dry they are sometimes sprinkled into sheep's head broth. Riddlebread was hung on the flakes of the inns for customers to take a piece as they wished.

When he was a lad living in Bowland, a farmer told us, his mother let the neigh-bours who hadn't a bakstone know when she was going to bake, and they came bringing their own meal. The following day any riddlebread which was to spare was sold at eighteen cakes for 1s. As a child he and the other children of the family were allowed to help, and competed as to who could make the best shaped cake.

Again, a farmer, who fifty years ago was a servant man at Low Trenhouse, near Malham Tarn, recollected the baking of oatcake there and that the mixture, made the night before, was marked with a cross on the surface as a charm against witches. In Malhamdale the Catons baked oatcake at Tennant House until just before the First World War. No one was allowed to stoke the fire except Mrs Caton. Similarly the Bollands at Malham, making oatcake, sold it at the price of two cakes for 1½d., four for 3d., eight for 6d. and sixteen for 1s.

In Wharfedale and Littondale Miss A. Ingleby baked oatcake for sale at Nether Hesleden and later at Kilnsey up to about twenty-five years ago. People came from miles away for it, and she always had a well-filled order book. Low Gamsworth, Barden, was formerly the scene of great baking days, and at Barden Scale, a bakstone still *in situ*, was used up to about 1940 by the Demaines. The face of the iron plate here was kept in good order by melted beeswax. Often it was greased with a piece of fat bacon.

Although recollections are on the whole scanty in Nidderdale, built-in bak-stones were in common use. Lucas writes of clapcake, riddlecake, *held-on cake* and *turn down cake*, of which the last three were made by pouring on to a bakstone. Here a commercial baker journeyed round selling his products, just as a similar baker called Heap is remembered journeying up Wharfedale from Grassington to sell oatcake, muffins and milk cakes.

Round Sedbergh, including Cautley, Howgill and Dent, and in the adjoining parts of Westmorland haverbread was baked with *havermeal* (oatmeal) as it was called there. In Howgill where oats were grown up to the First World War and in places during the Second, the traditional sequence of growing the corn, milling it and baking the havermeal into haverbread is remembered.

Mr E. Middleton of Davy Bank Mill on the Lune in Howgill recollects seeing as many as thirteen horses and carts waiting in the yard to deliver oats (and some-times barley) for grinding and to take back what had already previously been ground. Six hundredweights at a time, spread about six inches deep, were dried for five hours in the kiln heated with furnace coke. Turned with a wooden shovel by a miller wearing clogs or boots with thick soles, the oats were heated until too hot to hold, when they were ready. They then went twice through a pair of Derbyshire Peak stones, the first for shelling and the second for grinding and lastly through six layers of wire mesh riddles. The products were mill dust which fell through the riddles, the groats, used for havermeal, and the husks (called *how* seeds, *hulls* or *shools*) which weighing light were sent to Liverpool in large sacks for packing pottery to send abroad. Each farmer's corn was dealt with separately and was charged for at the rate of so much a stone. Some oats made fifty to fifty-five per cent to 100 stone, but the poor only made thirty to thirty-five per cent. Fresh ground havermeal made the best tasting haverbread, and the miller's father used to say 'it was no good if it hadn't fire in it'. Havermeal kept best when air was excluded, so that it was pressed down tight in the meal ark, sometimes by trampling with the feet.

Many if not most of the farmhouses in Dowbiggin, Cautley and Howgill had bakstones. Fifty or sixty years ago the farmer's wife set aside a day for baking. The ingredients consisted of havermeal, water and salt, kneaded to a dough rolled out thin into a round about twenty inches in diameter. This was rolled on to the turner, a long thin rolling pin, from which it was unrolled on to the bakstone, which had a hot and a cool end. First baked on the hot half, the haverbread was lifted and turned over with the fingers and sometimes a spittle on to the cool side. If need be the baker twisted it round with the flat of her hand.

Mr J. Postlethwaite, formerly of Riddings, Howgill, remembered, 'We were browt up on haverbreead and blue-milk cheese'. As children they always ate it for supper and were taught to eat politely by breaking off small pieces from the big round cake. Mrs R. Brunskill of Archers' Hall, Millthrop, near Sedbergh, tells us that her mother had a horsehair brush specially made from hairs from their white horse's tail, with which to sweep the bakstone clear of burnt bits of meal. She still has a huge meal ark (now filled with blankets) kept in the bedroom over the kitchen, as was the custom. It is divided into two compartments, and havermeal was kept in the larger side and wheatmeal in the smaller.

In both Langstrothdale and Dent it is remembered that rolled out cakes were made on the girdle. Betty Yewdale in Southey's *The Doctor* described the coarse food in Dent about 1760 as 'Round Meal an they *stoult* (threw roughly) it int' frying pan è keeaks as thick as my finger'. Mr W. Bayne remembers how at Lambparrocks in Dent his grandmother poured a small quantity of batter on to the girdle type bakstone, flipped it over with her fingers and hung it up to dry. It was then kept in drawers in the kitchen dresser—that in the top drawer was to eat, that in the second for drying, and that in the third had just been put in. It was often eaten with 'tatie hash'. But in both Dent and Langstrothdale, where methods and types of oatcake overlap, built-in bakstones existed.

In Swaledale and Wensleydale a wholly different picture appears. The implements used were a girdle-type bakstone, a wooden *cake stool*, and either a knife or a baking spittle for turning. (*See drawings on page* 23.) The bakstone, perhaps as large as seventeen inches in diameter, varied in size, and usually had a *bewl* (handle) with a swivelling ring at the top and sometimes an iron projection as handle. The latter rested on a *crow*, which Lucas called a *branderi*, that is, bars which spanned the fire, fixed on the front bar of the fire grate. 'I've thrown dozens of bakstones away,' says the retired Askrigg blacksmith, and scarcely a household was formerly without one. The cake stool, *cake dog*, jack or hod was very occasionally turned and ornamental, but, liable to be burnt, it was more often utilitarian in design.

Mrs J. Alderson, formerly of Stone House, upper Swaledale, has described the recipe and her daughter-in-law made havercake for us at Keld. Usually only oatmeal, water and salt were the ingredients, but some used buttermilk or even whey. Some dissolved a quantity of fat or dripping the size of a walnut in hot water for each cake; others in later days added a little bi-carbonate of soda. The stiff dough is difficult to roll out and only one cake is rolled at a time. Already hung over a bright peat fire, the bakstone was not greased, but a little of the dough was tried out on it for temperature. Then the havercake was transferred with the baking spittle on to the bakstone, which was moved up and down on the reckan or swivelled round to regulate the heat. After a minute or so the baker dexterously turned it with a knife. 'It used to be said', Mrs Alderson told us, 'that you weren't fit to get married until you could turn a havercake, and everyone took a pride in the thinness and shape.' Transferred to the stool in front of the fire to dry, it was then finally stored in the havercake scuttle (a basket). Or the cakes might be wrapped in a white cloth and stored on the ceiling boards of the kitchen.

Formerly a day was usually set aside before lambing, hay and sheep salving-times for baking havercake. It was eaten with butter and cheese and *crappins*, a product of rendering down pork fat. It put the children on between meals. A farmer set off on to the moor with pieces in his pocket, or coming home, broke a bit off and cut off a slice of raw bacon to lay on it to eat. When families after the failure of the lead-mines in Swaledale emigrated, they packed havercake in apple barrels to take with them across the 'Great Dub'. At Hawes fifty years ago children used to buy haverbread (as it was sometimes called there) broken up at 1½d. a poke from old Maggie Pritchard.

Time after time we have been told how people doted on oatcake. 'Mi father lived on oatcake' they say. Another explained than when her mother was carrying her sister, she craved for riddlebread. 'When she was born, Martha was covered wi' oatmeal.' 'Straight off t' bakstone' is a saying meaning 'off the cuff'.

Oatbread baking, of almost any variety, is a craft requiring skill, as anyone who tries his hand will discover. Oatcake keeps you warm, is sustaining and good for the teeth. Whenever it is mentioned people's eyes light up as they remember from their childhood the delicious smell on a baking day, the well-filled flake and the delectable taste of their favourite variety.

FARM BUILDINGS
& IMPLEMENTS

UNTIL recently dales' farms had on the whole few buildings. A full complement was a stable, cartshed, *hoghouse* (for young sheep), calf *hull*, pigsty, turf house and two or three cowhouses. Sheep were and are seldom indoors; horses were wintered on the pastures except for one or two kept in a stable for pulling a trap or for shepherding. Cows, however, indoors from the end of November until May, require cowhouses, which is a term synonymous in the dales with barn.

As we have said, a barn may well adjoin the farmhouse under the same roof, but in the dales' system of farming, unique so far as the writers are aware in the United Kingdom, most barns are some distance from the farmhouses situated so that the hay from the surrounding meadows may be stored in them in order to fodder the cows there in winter, and also for the convenient spreading of manure.[1]

They are variously called the cowhouse (cow'us), field house and *lathe*. Field house, a term found in Swaledale and the dales farther north, defines a barn away from the house.[2] The name for the actual cowshed is *shippon* in many parts of Craven, *mistal* in Nidderdale and at Grassington in Wharfedale and byre in Baldersdale.

Those in Craven, particularly in Wharfedale and Littondale, are in general much larger, with porches and double doors, and of much more interest architecturally than the simpler smaller ones of the North Riding dales. The double doors enable carts to be drawn inside to unload hay, and they open on to what was the threshing bay with cow standings on either side. There are *outshuts* (lean-to additions) for calf hulls and dog kennels, and sometimes a pigeon cote in the porch. The few barns of cruck construction round Barden in Wharfedale, form a group in themselves, and, once ling-thatched but now covered with corrugated iron sheeting, they are fascinating relics.

In the North Riding dales the lathe is usually no more than a two-storied oblong building often with two single doors, one leading into the cowshed with four

[1] See *Farm Life in a Yorkshire Dale* by W. H. Long and G. M. Davies (1948), p. 26.
[2] For the distribution of various terms see *Transactions of the Yorkshire Dialect Society*, vol. XI, part LXII (cowhouse) and vol. XI, part LXV (lathe).

standings and the other into the hay mow and with a forking-hole high up through which the hay is forked into it. Both types have features in common: the standings for the cows, the hay mow, and the *balks*—the loft or lofts above the cows where hay is also stored.

In Wensleydale round Redmire and Castle Bolton the even smaller single-storied barns have room only for the cows. Hay, formerly made into stacks, (lumps and *stamps* of hay appear in early inventories) is housed in small Dutch barns adjoining.[1] This type of barn, once much more general, belonged to miners' smallholdings.

Each part of a cowhouse has a name originating from the Norse and Danish settlers, and varying only slightly from dale to dale (*see plates 53–60 and illustrations on page 33*). The *booses* (standings) were partitioned in pairs by large upended rounded flagstones, which were sunk almost their full height into the ground and by similar smaller flagstones in between these. Except for the *settlestones* the booses were paved with cobblestones. Cows lie down by kneeling first. In upper Swaledale we are told that they experienced less trouble with cows' knees on the pavings than on the present-day smooth concrete. Yet in Baldersdale it was customary to place *benty* sods at the boose head to soften the impact of kneeling.

In this dale ancient barns are remembered with sod lofts, that is with the balks constructed of rough beams, crossed with birch sticks and covered with sods. Here, when the barn stood on a steep hillside, the door to the hay mow had of necessity to be on the upper floor, and the space for the hay was called a *sink mew*.

Cows are fastened to the iron ring on the *ridstake* or *rudster* by a chain, or a cowband, which is now a rope fastened by a loop and *clog* (toggle). The iron ring[2] was formerly of twisted withy, and the cowband a hazel bow, which, threaded through the ring and placed round the cow's neck, was fastened by a wooden catch resting on the neck behind the horns (*see illustration on page 33*). The method, once general in many parts of Britain, is almost forgotten in the dales.

[1] The inventory of the goods of William Hirde, Arkengarthdale in 1681 mentions ' 2 stamps of hay'.

[2] The iron ring is called a *round bank* in Dent, Littondale, upper Ribblesdale, and at Buckden and Kettlewell, Wharfedale. It is a *widdie* in Nidderdale, a *runner* in upper Wensleydale and a *redwiddie* at Grassington, Wharfedale, and in Craven.

SPADES AND FORKS

1 Paring or flaying spade, 7 ft long, front view. 1a Paring or flaying spade, side view showing wing. 2 Tom spade. 3 Gripping spade (Baldersdale). 4 Gripping spade (Malhamdale). 5 Draining scoop. 6 Scaling fork for scaling muck. 7 Cowling rake for raking muck out from cart. 8 Mucking rake for raking muck with bedding in it out from cart. 9 Draining spade. 10 Hay knife. 11 Hay spade (old type). 12 Hay spade (modern) used from the front. 13 Turf spade (Skipton Museum) used for taking turfs from the top of the peat pot.

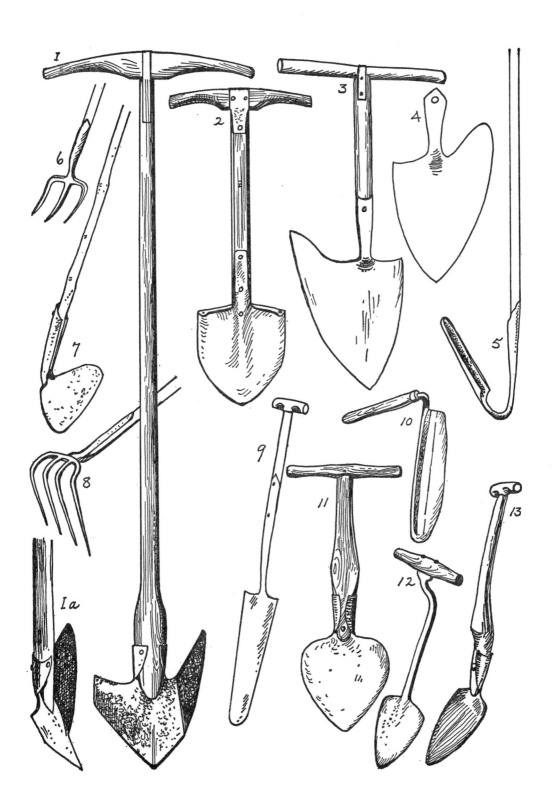

In every barn a milking *coppy* (stool) and pail, formerly wooden, were essential, and a backcan, described in the chapter on dairy work, was used to carry the milk from barn to farmhouse. There were two ling besoms made either by the farmer or bought in dozens from a besom maker. One was kept for brushing hay seeds from the boose head into the *group* and the other for cleaning the group from which the manure was thrown out of the mucking hole by a shovel. A drenching horn hung from a hook, witchstones over the door, and other small objects were stored in small open compartments always to be found in barn walls.

Hay spades were necessary in the mew or *mewstead* as it is sometimes called. The squares of hay left by cutting are called *desses*, whilst the layer of hay lifted off is a *canch*, a term which we have heard in Swaledale only. At farms in the dales radiating from Hawes, made there by the ropemaker or on the farm, a pair of creels for carrying hay short distances was always found, and in Swaledale burden ropes hung from a nail at the back of the hay mew door. A story relates: 'A dalesman when in London went to one o' them big stores as sells owt fra a needle tiv a steeam engine. They said, "Anything you want, we'll supply". The dalesman asked for a *stee* (ladder) for t'balks an' a pair o' creels. That finished 'em.'

Mr W. Hunter, Crow Trees, Swaledale, has made us a pair of creels and shown us how a burden was made (*see plates* 63–8 *and* 70–3). Two burdens, slung on either side of the horse's back, were a means of transporting hay long distances to sheep on the moor. The burdens had to be equal in weight, and if they were not they were balanced by tucking a stone under the rope of the lighter one. Having arrived at his destination, the farmer removed the wisp of hay holding the knot and the rope fell off. 'You want to be quick, when you've tweea thri hundred hungry sheep coming at you.' Many a time Mr Hunter has tied all the hay of a large field house into burdens—a hard job often undertaken after foddering at night until supper time. 'I've made manny a thousand.'

Another job, mucking, meant carrying the manure from the heap outside the barn to lay it on the meadows. A horse and cart or *coup*, *cowl-rake* and *gripe* (muck-fork) were used, (*shown on plates* 61–2 *and drawings on pages* 31 *and* 34). Raked out in heaps suitably spaced apart, the muck was then *scaled* (spread) with the gripe. When casual labour was available in the past, a farmer if he could afford it let out all his mucking either by the day or at $\frac{1}{2}$d. a heap, a sum which increased to 1d. thirty years ago. The manure was carefully spread to distribute it evenly, and, fanned out from each heap, it was thrown in a half circle and rubbed thin with the gripe. Lastly, it was harrowed by a horse pulling an oblong wooden framework, crossed with thin branches and weighted with stones, so that the bushy ends of the branches spread the manure. Later a chain harrow was used.

Implements were few; those connected with haymaking are described later.

19. *The dairy at West Park, Cotherstone, showing cheese on traves (cheese shelves), butter, cream cheeses, honey, and cream bowls* (c. *1915*).

20 *Mrs W. Birkett, West Park, and helpers pouring curds into the cheese trough* (c. *1915*).

21. *Mrs W. Birkett putting curds into a cheese vat* (c. *1939*).

CHEESE MAKING

CHEESE PRESSES

22. *Iron cheese press: Mrs P. Metcalfe, Shoregill, Swaledale.*

23. *Wooden cheese press used for generations by the Keartons of Thwaite, Swaledale. The wooden bar was drawn down on to the chesford by cranking the round wooden wheel and then a stone weight was suspended from the crook on the bar.*

24. *Two cheese presses at Hill Top Farm, Swaledale. Mrs R. J. Guy demonstrates screwing down the wooden bar. This press was regularly used up to a few years ago and both were used forty years ago.*

25. *Cheese press, formerly in the porch at Gill Head, Oxnop, Swaledale.*

26. Mrs W. E. Iceton demonstrates churning with a stand churn, formerly used in Baldersdale by the Hawkswell family.

◁

27. Mrs W. Mason, Lodge Hall, Ribblesdale, churning with an end-over-end churn.

28. Miss E. Alderson, Black Howe, Swaledale, churns with a table churn.

29. Mrs T. J. Middleton, Gawthrop, Dent, demonstrates a butter-worker belonging to the Capsticks of Tofts, Gawthrop. It squeezes out the water.

BUTTER MAKING

▷

30. *After churning, Miss E. Alderson clashes the butter in a wooden bowl to remove the buttermilk.*

31. *Mrs W. Mason, having weighed the butter into pounds, has rolled one into a cone, ready for printing.*

32. *Mrs W. Mason making up into round pounds. Note the round marker on the left.*

33. *Mrs Lily Simpson, Westfield, Nidderdale, has rolled her butter sideways on a large board and is marking the rolls with a roller-marker.*

14. *Miss E. Carr mixing the batter for riddlebread at a farmhouse near Bentham.*

15. *Baking on the bakstone. A ladle hangs in the pail containing the batter, and a ladleful, about ¼ of a pint, is put in the basin and poured in a pool on the bakstone. Note the pile of riddlebread in right bottom corner.*

16. *The pool of batter is thinned out with the scraper which has two screws in the base which determine the thickness and width of the cake.*

17. *After loosening with a knife, the cake is lifted with the baking spittle, ready to turn.*

18. *Turning the cake, holding it with the left hand against the baking spittle.*

19. *Riddlebread drying, hung across two strings on the flake.*

▷

BAKING
HAVERCAKE

20. *Baking havercake. One is baking on the bakstone and the other drying on the cake stool.*

21. *Mrs J. Alderson, Keld, Swaledale, prepares to turn the havercake on the bakstone. A second cake is drying on the cake stool.*

42. *A bread flake at Arches Farm, Bolton Abbey. They were not usually painted. Soft oatcake was hung to dry over the lats.*

43. *A bakstone in what is now an outhouse, Low Haycote, Gawthrop, Dent. The fireplace, ornamented with wreaths of leaves in high relief, dates from about 1800 and has fire-boxes under both oven and boiler. This old kitchen has a large stone cheese press in a recess and a slopstone. The bakstone has a ventilating shaft to the left of it.*

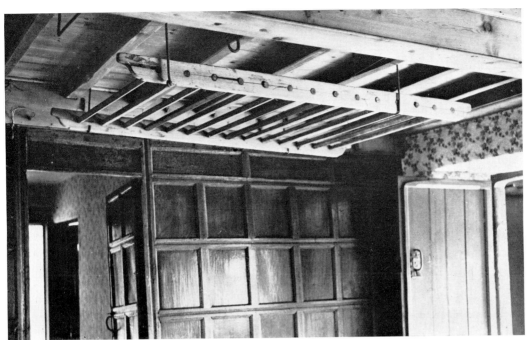

44. *A bacon flake at Stone House, Upper Swaledale. The Welsh Car Eig Moch. After pig killing in November or December the hams, sides and shoulders of bacon were laid on it for two or three months.*

FLAKES, & BAKSTONES IN KITCHENS

45. *A bakstone of the Sedbergh type on the right of the photograph, in a recess in the kitchen at Alderson Spout, Dowbiggin. It was taken out in 1965.*

KNITTING & SPINNING

46. *Mrs M. Dinsdale, one of the la[*]
*of the old knitters, and her family a[*]
Appersett, Wensleydale (c. 1949).

47. *Knitter and traveller on the roa[*]
*side in Dent. Wood engraving by S[*]
Williams from The Rural Life o[*]
England *by William Howitt (1844[*]

48. *Mr D. Durham and spinnin[*]
*wheel, Aysgarth, Wensleydale (c. 1890[*]

QUILTING

49. *Mrs C. Alderson, Eleanor an[*]
*Jennifer, Black Howe Farm, Swaledale[*]
*working a quilt and stitching traditiona[*]
patterns

50. *Mrs H. Kirkbride, Town Head Farm, Askrigg, Wensleydale, making a hooky rug.*

RUG MAKING

51. *The Swindlehurst family, Brackengarth, Keasden, plucking geese for sale at Lancaster market* (C. *1910*).

PLUCKING GEESE & STRIPPING FEATHERS

52. *Mrs J. Postlethwaite, Riddings, Howgill, stripping feathers for pillows* (C. *1940*).

53. *Barns at Castle Bolton, Wensleydale.*

54. *Littondale Barn.*

55. *Swaledale Barn.*

56. *Moor Close Farm, Swaledale, showing the disposition of four barns in the meadows.*

BARNS

57. *Barn in Baldersdale with what was originally a sod loft and primitive stone boskins (partitions).*

58. *Banks Laithe, Grassington, with oak boskins.*

CRUCK-BUILT BARN & PAVINGS

59. *Barn at Drebley, Wharfedale, showing a cruck and spars for ling thatch.*

60. *Paved floor of barn at Rash, Dent, also showing settlestones.*

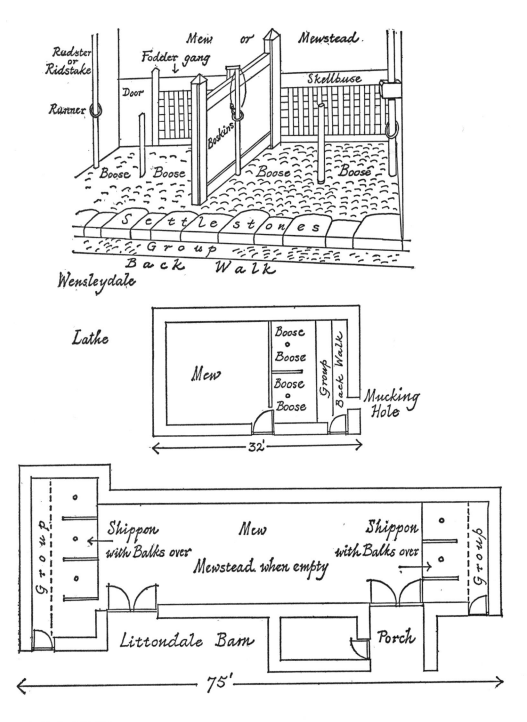

Rudster
or
Ridstake

Runner

Mew   or   Mewstead.

Fodder gang

Door

Skellbuse

Boskins

Boose   Boose   Boose   Boose

S e t t l e   s t o n e s
G r o u p
B a c k   W a l k

Wensleydale

Lathe

Mew

Boose
o
Boose

Boose
o
Boose

Group

Back Walk

Mucking
Hole

← 32' →

Group

Shippon
with Balks over

Mew

Mewstead. when empty

Shippon
with Balks over

Group

Littondale Barn

Porch

← 75' →

COW HOUSE

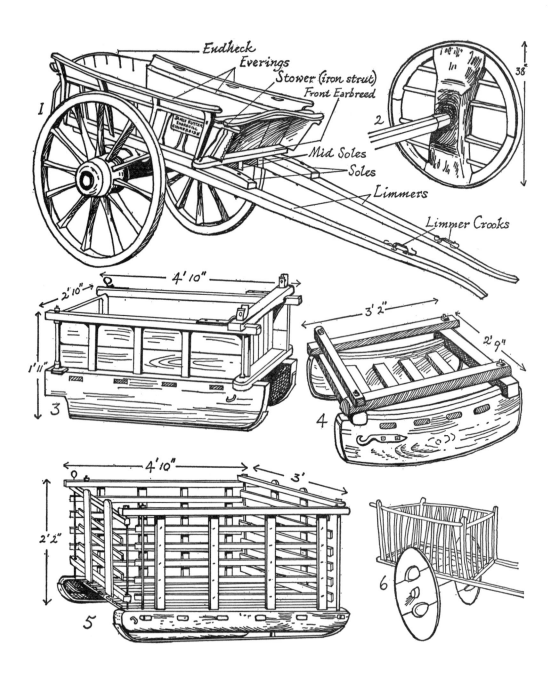

Endheck
Everings
Stower (iron strut)
Front Earbreed
Mid Soles
Soles
Limmers
Limmer Crooks

38″

CARTS

1 Swaledale cart, probably made at Muker. 2 Clog wheel from Sedbergh (Bowes Museum). 3 Coup. 4 Stone sled, used for carrying stone for building and for clearing the land, made by Clark's, Burnsall, Wharfedale. 5 Peat cart used at Stone House, Keld, Swaledale. 6 Peat cart from Walker's Costume of Yorkshire.

Primitive carts, called tumble cars, had clog-wheels which revolved with the axle to which the body was pegged (*see drawing of wheel on page* 34).[1] It used to be said when starting off on a journey in Dent, 'Take a peg anthers', (in case a peg broke). Carts, usually on the small side and two-wheeled, included ones which tipped or were fixed, or ones with loose shelvings, or latterly milk floats were used for transporting kits of milk to the stations. A high or tub trap was kept by larger farmers for journeys to market.

The coup cart or trail coup with runners not wheels and now almost obsolete was occasionally employed for carrying in general. It was especially efficacious in snow, when it slid easily over the hard frozen surface. Mr Hunter remembers that in the winter of 1895 coups were the only vehicles which reached Thwaite, in Swaledale, for eight or nine weeks, and that goods were fetched in them from Askrigg Station, in Wensleydale. When used on steep hillsides, shafts could be fitted, so that the horse had more control than when it was harnessed to the coup by the usual ropes or chains. Stone sleds for carting stone for building resembled coups.

A chamber over stable, cowhouse or cartshed was sometimes floored with flags, and was and is utilized as a general workshop with a bench and vice for making sticks, repairing implements, and so on. Here if it was large enough, space was cleared for dances on outlying farms far from the long rooms of the inns, when the men were dressed up if they put on a clean *kitle* (overall coat) and when the local fiddler provided the music.

Besides the new goods—the tins of dipping compound, the syringes, the ear-markers and so on—a chamber may still contain a collection of the small often outmoded implements of a dales' farm (*see illustrations on pages* 31, 41, 109). A single farm might not have possessed all of these; but meal arks, rakes, pitchforks, a scythe or two together with sharpening equipment, and outside in a paddock a grindstone, were common to all.

Much of the old system has been superseded. Milking parlours are being built near the farmhouses, doing away with the field houses in the meadows. Bales of hay have replaced burdens and the use of pairs of creels, and muck spreaders have done away with the laborious carting and scaling of muck.

---

[1] See *Transactions of the Yorkshire Dialect Society*, vol. XI, part LXIV. 'Clog Wheels' by F. Atkinson and A. Ward.

SHEEP

ALTHOUGH the stock on dales' farms are mixed, sheep predominate on the highland farms, and sheep lore, as might be expected, is paramount. The breeds of Swaledale, Dalesbred and Rough derive from the indigenous stock of the fells, and each flock knows its own *heugh* (North Riding), *heaf* (West Riding), like the Icelandic *hefta* meaning to restrain. A farm may have three or four heughs on the open moorland where the lambs have grown up with their mothers; and heughed sheep are sold with the farm. Tupping and lambing times, washing (now discontinued), shearing, *spaining* (separating the lambs from the ewes), salving (now converted to dipping), occupied and occupy the farmer throughout the year.

Counting sheep with the ancient sheep-scoring numerals has gone.[1] Mr C. H. Lister, born 1902 at Skyreholme, Wharfedale, says that his father heard William Demaine of Barden Scale using them, and that each time he reached twenty he doubled a finger down, and finally the thumb, so counting 100.

Except on certain fells the farmer, continually 'among t' sheep', is his own shepherd and, even calling some by name, he knows almost every member of the flock by its gait, looks and markings. Formerly, some sheep were branded on the nose or side of the face to identify them, a practice which turned the hair white where burnt. But the traditional and official marks are published in the *Shepherds Guides*. That for the northern Pennines contains some 1,500 farmers' marks. These —horn burns, wool and ear marks—go with the farm and the initials burnt on the horn often refer to a farmer living there years ago.

Mr W. G. Wallbank of Rantree, Keasden, near Clapham, has told us the following strange story of recognizing a sheep. They once had some stolen at a fair, and their shepherd, called as a witness against the thief, said that he could swear to knowing one of the stolen animals in 10,000. At first the judge was sceptical. But he was told that when the sheep was born, the shepherd had been out on the pastures, and seeing a carrion crow circling round he had hurried down to find the lamb partly born with its head swollen and almost half of its tongue pecked away.

[1] *Studies in Nidderdale* by Joseph Lucas, p. 37–40. *Transactions of the Yorkshire Dialect Society*, no. XXVIII (1927). *The Dalesman*, vol. II., nos. 11 and 12.

The shepherd saved the lamb's life, but its tongue was permanently damaged. The sheep was brought into court and the tongue shown to the jury, who were only out a few minutes before finding a verdict of Guilty.

Washing sheep, which gradually ended early in the twentieth century, took place in late June. Formerly a slightly better price was paid for washed wool, and inter-linked with salving it rid the fleece of the salve. Washfold is both a place-name and a name for the actual folds, usually three—large, small and catchers' folds—still to be found by becks on the moorlands or by rivers near to many villages.

If a natural dub did not exist, neighbouring farmers went the day before to dam the beck either with planks or an embankment of stones, with the crevices stuffed with sods. Washings, like clippings, were festive occasions to which relations, friends and their children resorted, and at which food and drink followed by games and sports were enjoyed. At the Stean washings in Nidderdale rabbit pies were popular and at others one man might bring rum, another gin, and another whisky. At Beckermonds, Langstrothdale, mulled ale, made from ale, milk and eggs, was popular. 'Washings were allus meeade a lot on.'

Mr Gilbert Brown (1886–1966) of Malham described sheep-washing. 'You could make a dub anywhere if you had the folds. There were three dubs at Malham: Beck Hole, Jennet Foss, and at the west of the village on Cove road. You started to wash early, and were finished by two o'clock. You had a mouthful or two of whisky to start with, and sometimes in between, but nothing to eat until you had finished. The dub was about four feet deep; and although you were up to your armpits in the water, you soon got warm and wore no special clothes. If the water goes down your neck, then you feel the cold. There would perhaps be two men washing. Never put a sheep in head first or it will splash. There were men on the bank who threw them in bottom first. It could but come to you. You collared 'em anywhere by a bit o' wool, put one hand over the neck to hold it, and gave it a good *dolly* on both sides. Then you turned the sheep over in the water by putting one arm under its neck and the other on its loin. By pressing, it came over easily. It was dollied again, and then done the same the other way. Its head was always above water. If the sheep just swam through, it did good. Swimming was very near as good as washing. When we'd done, we had a big meal brought to the wash place about two or three o'clock. We made a party of it.'

Another description of washing was given us by Mr Thomas Joy who attended those on Blea Beck on Grassington Moor. They started gathering at nine o'clock. The big fold held 1,000 sheep, which were let through into the next and finally into the small catcher's fold. Each sheep was thrown in by two men standing on the bank one at each side of the gate. They held on to the wool of the breast and buttocks, and threw so that the sheep landed in the water on its back. The washers grabbed the animal by the forelegs, dollied it, particularly the belly and tail. As they swam across, the dirt floated out.

Mr G. Metcalfe, Bouthwaite, Nidderdale, said that there were two or three of you standing in the dub. Old rags were worn, but you were careful to tie up sleeves so that the water couldn't get in. They swam towards you head first. You washed the belly with your hands, then one side with the forearm using from hand to elbow, turned them, and washed the other side. After their heads were dipped in, they swam off.

'Although they thowt nowt about it, an hour and a half to an hour and three quarters was long enough to be in the water', says Mr Jonathan Graham of Nidderdale. 'The pay was 5s. You wore two pairs of old trousers and a bag tied round you, and if you stood in one place, the water near you was warmer. You should never be kept waiting. The throwers should send another sheep towards you just as you are finishing one. When you come out, you always changed into dry clothes.' It was ill advised to go in a second time, as Mr J. Swales of Nidderdale once did and contracted sciatica.

In Bowland and Keasden men wore special washing suits. At Cow Dub, in Dent, where 3,000 were washed at a time, 'they lapped thersels i' fleeces all round their bodies and legs, and tied them on'. Afterwards not one lamb went to the wrong mother. In upper Ribblesdale and in other places the washers stood in forty-gallon barrels weighted down with stones.

Washing encouraged the growth of the *rise*, the new wool which lifts the fleece from the skin of a sheep, and the state of which largely determines the right time for clipping, which usually took place about ten days after washing. Machine clipping is at present practised on only a few farms in the dales. Except for the *bow* (handle), the pattern of sheep shears has remained unaltered since Roman times, and is the same for *cuddies*, left-handed people, as for right. Nowadays a farmer manages his clippings with the aid of a son, farmhand, or neighbours; but formerly like the washings this event was an occasion for large gatherings.

Mr Gilbert Brown remembers that when he was working at Lamb Hill, Bowland, they used to shear 1,000 sheep in a day. There might be eighty to ninety men and many women helping, the latter providing snacks and a meal at the end. The farmer sent word round; and men came from four or five miles away. Some rode, some walked. Some were sent out to gather the flocks, which were brought down in separate lots. Others started clipping, others acted as wrappers, catchers and sharpeners. The work took place indoors, where the men sat on *stocks* (stools) along both sides of a large barn and the sheep came down the middle.

When shorn, you let them go, and they went out at the end. As each sheep passed, two men posted at the door dabbed them with tar marks; 'they never touched 'em.' Beer and snacks were on the go all the time; and at the end of the day the men washed in a long trough of water with cakes of soap set out at intervals. They then went in to a hot meal of roast beef—roast anything. There were barrels of beer—some had a bit too much. Afterwards the fiddlers and a concertina player started up, and there was dancing until dawn, 't' same sort o' dancing as now, only done a bit different—quadrilles, lancers and waltzes'.

In this region of large sheep farms the tradition of great gatherings was general. Mr W. G. Wallbank remembers stories of his mother's day at Keasden Head. Ninety people used to come to their clipping day, when over 1,000 sheep were clipped. There might be forty clippers, also catchers, lappers and the women preparing the food. At night they celebrated with as much drink as they wanted, and the music of a trombone, fiddle and concertina.

People used to enjoy clipping days and were hurt if they were left out. 'I found t' best way was to arrange a day, and then tell as many as I could, "You'll all be welcome".' Mr Wallbank recalls, 'I've seen twenty-two men clipping in a line. You should be in a straight line lest the shears fly. I once went to a clip in Maller-stang, and instead of joining the men in a row I began against a barn door. "Nay, lad," said the farmer, "if you're going to clip here you'll have to do as we do"—to which I replied, "I'm here to be told".'

At Spanham between Arkengarthdale and Teesdale they worked all day and in the dark by the light of candles stood on the wall top, and after playing nap by the fire until about 6 a.m., called in at Stang End public house on the way home.

Many of the farmers round Bowes and on Stainmore still have special clipping days to which ten or more clippers resort. In the past practical jokes, such as the sewing up of coats, enlivened the monotony; and it is still traditional at Stang Foot Farm to provide plum puddings, of which five or six are made the week before, to follow the meat course.[1] Howitt writes of huge mutton pies seasoned with cur-rants, raisins, candied peel and sugar, gooseberry pies and curd cheesecakes.[2] Gooseberry and raisin pies used always to be made for the washings by Mrs J. Beckwith.

A generation ago everyone clipped sitting on a stool. Nowadays although no hard and fast rule is observed, it is usual to stand up on a sheet to keep the wool clean. For a man growing older and not so *lish* standing, however, may be a back-breaking job.

The stool was in fact the greasing stool on which sheep were formerly salved— a much longer, slower process than clipping, which 'you can snap away at'. Although the terms overlap, it is called a stock in Dent and Bowland, a *cratch* in

[1] Mr J. Addison, Stoney Keld, near Bowes.
[2] *The Rural Life of England*, by William Howitt (1837).

STOOLS, BARROWS, etc.

1 Peat barrow. 2 Peat barrow wheel made of wood and a 2-in. iron tyre. 3 Drag rake. 4 Greasing stool. 5 Salving bowl. 6 Salving bowl. 7 Stool made from forked tree. 8 Pig stool used at pig-killing time. 9 Sheep cratch (Wensleydale). 10 Two-man barrow.

Wensleydale and upper Ribblesdale, a stock and cratch in Wharfedale and a *creel* in Howgill and Teesdale. An early type was made by sawing a forked tree trunk in half. (*See drawings on page* 41). When his family left Keasden Head, Mr W. G. Wallbank remembers that they found thirty-two stocks, some of them of the forked type, in an attic. Mr R. Bayne, joiner at the Weaving Shops, Cowgill, Dent, made stocks for 7s. 6d. each fifty years ago. They should be well curved. 'A right good sheep stock doesn't catch the legs.' The greasing stools usually had the back legs set closer together than those used later for clipping only.

Clippers sitting on stools and those standing up observe different methods (*for both of these see plates* 79–83 *and* 89). The man who stands up clips right and then left from the neck downwards as far as he may comfortably reach; next he kneels on one knee to clip first one side and then the other, finishing with the tail.

We have attended many sheep shearings over the years, when the talk turns on marks, horn-burns, teeth, ages, favourite sheep and the like. Nowadays no one ever sees sheep *keds* (lice), which have been killed off by modern dips. The hogs are always finished first. 'If t' hogs are bad to clip, it's a puer do.' Men have been known to give the catcher 1d. to persuade them to bring them the ones with a good rise. A poor one, often left to the end, can take twenty minutes to clip. Sometimes when the wool has *sliped* off during the spring, a sheep is said to have 'clipped itself'. Three and a half minutes a sheep is quick work.

To be speedy the wrapper must also be skilful. The *doddings* (North Riding) or *gowdings* (West Riding), the dirty locks round the tail, are kept separate, and the fleece lapped tightly in a roll with the dark outside wool inside and a length of neck wool twisted round with elbow and forearm, brought tightly round the roll and tucked in. Some men made wrapping their speciality, and boast that they could keep up with twenty-two clippers.

Formerly a major task amongst the sheep in the autumn, salving, or 'sorving' as it is usually pronounced, was undertaken in October and finished before tupping time. It consisted of smearing the skin of a sheep all over with a mixture of oils, fats and tar to kill parasites and to prevent scab. *Sheddings* (partings) were systematically made in the wool in stripes at intervals of about an inch, in a specific sequence. One sheep took fifty minutes to an hour to salve. In 1298/99 an entry in the accounts of Bolton Priory reads: 'Oil, tallow and tar used for smearing the sheep £4 10s. 7½d.' *General View of Agriculture* (1794) gives: '1 gallon of tar and 17 lb. of butter which serves from 25 to 30 sheep.' In September salve manufacturers and those who sold the ingredients in barrels attended markets and fairs.

It took many years for the old practice to die out. Francis Garth of Haverdale, Swaledale, changed over to dipping in 1857, whilst others, who believed that salving formed a valuable protective coating for winter, went on until a compulsory dipping order came into force in 1905. Elderly men remember helping as boys, patiently stirring the mixture, being allowed to do the tails, or wrapping a rag daubed with salve round their forefingers to blacken them and make it appear that they were engaged in grown-up work. Young men on the other hand were ashamed of their blackened fingers at dances. 'You could allus ken a salver by his first finger, which was as brown as a berry.'

Mr Frank Graham of Grimes Gill between Masham and Middlesmoor says that his father and uncle used to go salving in Dallowgill and kept a record of what they were paid. To salve fifteen was a good day's work; if you did more you 'did 'em rough'. His father used to say: 'A strong man could just carry a salve pan when it was full'; and in old age his 'salving finger' was unusually flexible.

Mr E. Campbell, who was brought up at Cosh, Littondale, remembers that about sixty years ago whilst he was still at school, he helped his father to salve. 'We were t' last ter salve up here, and we oftens went on all night. My! I did get sleepy. My sister held cannles; and when we got a double-wicked lamp, it was a lot better. First when I was eight or nine I helped him salve part o' t' sheep, and when I was eleven or twelve and could hod 'em, I salved 'em all. Yes, I went to scule next day. I was no worse for it. Yer finger used to get varra black. Eh! teacher didn't like it. There was some white tar, and if you used it, it cleaned off t' black. T' salve were made of Stockholm tar and Danish butter. We sawed an apple barrel in half just bi t' bung-hole and poured in tar and stirred it. My! it was hard work. It was stiff. Then you heated t' butter in a big pan, not boiling, but hot, and that added to the tar made it less hard. Yer stirred until midnight.'

Mr John and Mr Richard Wallbank of upper Ribblesdale have described and demonstrated for us the process of salving as carried out some sixty years ago on their father's farm, High Grain, Eldroth, near Austwick, in Craven. The salve was made about a week before it was required in a pan on an outside fire. Although it could be bought ready-made, it was not always satisfactory. Their father always mixed his own from Archangel tar, whale oil, Brown George (which was old fat and oil out of fleeces), and buttermilk, which took the fire out of the tar and also helped the salve to spread better. The proportions were two thirds grease to one third tar. If too much tar was included, it burnt the sheep's skin.

In their childhood four helpers, farmers' sons or old men who lived in, were hired and stayed for a month from about 5th October. The sheep had to be dry, so the work was carried out in a barn or under a barn porch. Each man sat on a greasing stool with a wooden dish (bowl or pan) fixed by its handle under the side of the stool through a large staple. Salving bowls may be square but are usually round like small butter bowls. In the dish besides the salve was a *scrapple*, a wooden tool to scrape out the mixture. On the other side of the stool a man might have a buffet or box on which to put his pipe and tobacco. The half apple barrel containing the general stock of salve was kept in another building in case the sheep should knock it over.

First the sheep is placed on its back on the stool and the belly salved, if by a right-handed salver on the right first, then the middle, then the left, in sheddings here about two inches apart, elsewhere an inch. The neck is salved next. Then the two front legs and one hind leg are tied together to prevent struggling, and, with the sheep's tail near the salver, five sheddings are made and salved on the tail, and the back legs and buttocks finished with short cross-wise sheddings to meet at the top of the tail. Next, the legs are untied and the sheep is turned right-side up, head to the salver, and with its four legs dangling between the bars of the stool, so that it can't stir. Now all the back and sides are done by making sheddings from the neck nearest the salver to the top of the tail. The salve is put on the opposite way beginning at the tail end and ending with the neck. Next, three sheddings are made and salved across the *topping*; then the face, roots of the horns, and ears are rubbed. Lastly the salver ' *kems* 'em down' i.e. combs the wool away from himself three times with the outspread fingers and thumbs of both hands, and to distinguish which have been salved he marks the sheep by rubbing the wool between two stones smeared with red rud and grease.

If the farmer did not trust a salver, perhaps on Friday, pay day, when the work might be scamped, he examined the sheep. Often to avoid disputes the men put red or blue marks on different parts of the ear so that if a sheep were not well done, it was known who had salved it. The salve spreading and merging together formed a coat, which was lifted from the skin by the rise of the wool. Salved sheep were often put on fresh pastures to encourage the rise.

The Wallbanks have their ancestor's, Thomas Wallbank's, ledger covering the 1830's to the 1880's. Amongst the entries salve butter is sold at 6d. per lb. geese at 5s. and 4s. delivered, men servants hired for £10 a year, the number of 'sheep shorne' recorded, and, the most comprehensive entries, the records of the salving of their 500 to 600 sheep in four lots, ewes, hogs, wethers, and aged, from four heafs. Salving 510 sheep represented some 400 man-hours.

It is remembered that at High Grain, besides passing the time gossiping and smoking, a system of 3d. fines, with which to buy a bottle of whisky to drink afterwards, was customary. Not all are recollected, but some were for the following offences: if you hit a sheep or in any way lost your temper with it; if you ran out of salve in your dish before finishing a sheep; if you didn't scrape the dish clean before filling it up again; if you swore; and if you let the sheep escape. Afterwards they played nap for matchsticks, and might win a box or two in a night.

Sheep, although subject to many diseases, are very tough and have extraordinary powers of survival. When overblown in a sudden snowstorm, they may live for weeks, perhaps sheltering under a *brot* (overhang of peat hag), eating every particle of herbage round them and sometimes their own wool. They often come out with their wool quite white. 'As long as a sheep keeps on its feet, it's all right. Once it's laid down, it's all owered wi' it,' says Mr Joy. In the early part of this century William Pratt of Lunds and Garsdale once found a sheep after it had been overblown forty-nine days, and by giving it a very little to eat at first—a drop of milk and a little hay—it survived. Every farmer can tell stories of searching for and driving home sheep in a storm, calling to them 'Oh-ho! Oh-ho!' 'Howe! Howe!' or other calls depending on the district.

SHEEPDOGS

IT is thought that Border Collies were gradually introduced into northern England from Scotland, before the coming of railways, by the drovers a hundred and fifty or more years ago, and that the name may be derived from a Scottish breed of sheep, the 'coalie'.[1] Yet, easily within living memory the old rough sheepdog, with a 'bit of retriever in him', was still at work on dales' farms. Mr G. H. Capstick, Howgill, Sedbergh, tells us that in his father's time, even when collies had begun to be popular in the dales, sheepdogs were bred locally and there was no thought of pedigrees. The old 'bearded dogs', as Mr T. Lancaster, Artlegarth, Ravenstonedale, calls them, were often tan and different colours, with more hair on them, and given to barking they were good guard dogs. Extremely tough, they could run over the fells eight to ten hours at a stretch without tiring, and, heughed to the land like the sheep, if sold to a new owner living some distance away they often returned over the hills to their previous homes.

The older type of sheepdog was loose in its work, and did not concentrate on individual sheep like the 'eye' dogs[2] of today. These, the present-day sheepdogs, are pedigree black and white—often line-bred—Border Collies, and between the ages of nine months and a year they begin to 'eye and instinctively gather sheep'. Although the majority of farmers use these dogs on the farm, there are increasingly a group of men and their well-trained dogs worth £200 or more, competing in local, national and international sheepdog trials. Three of these expert handlers, the late Mr J. L. Peacock, Arkengarthdale, Mr T. Lancaster, Ravenstonedale, and Mr G. H. Capstick, Howgill have told us their methods.

A comment on Mr Peacock is that 'he was an artist amongst dogs'. He himself once told us: 'I was bred at Punchard [a well-known Arkengarthdale sheep farm with some three or four hundred breeding ewes], and as a schoolboy I used to get into trouble with my father for taking dogs along the walls for rabbits.' He went on: 'A dog should be one's friend; he must be taught through kindness, but he

[1] *The British Sheepdog* by Sidney Moorhouse (1950). *The Field*, 8th September, 1966, 'Of Shepherds, Dogs and Sheep' by F. W. Hill.
[2] Dogs which control the sheep with their eyes.

must be punished if he does wrong. A good dog's punishment is not to have pleased you. He'll know. He must learn to understand a situation and use his own brains. Dogs have intuitive minds and a great understanding may be established between a dog and his master. Some you can be severe with, some you can't, but you must be the boss.' Another time, Mr T. Lancaster said, 'You must treat your dog as you would treat your wife', and again Mr Capstick remarked: 'If you're in a bad temper, you'd best take your dog back to his kennel.'

In the past, dales' sheepdogs were controlled by shouted commands, but today these have been almost entirely replaced by a series of whistles which, depending on the wind, can carry up to a mile over the moors. Mr Lancaster thinks the best plan is to teach a dog both, because if it is too cold to whistle (the fingers, two of which are placed in the mouth, become numb) the commands, such as 'Way here' (go left) and 'Come by' (go right) may be used instead.

When a dog starts to 'eye', which shows he or she is ready to be trained, the first move is to 'put a line [lead] on him', and as Mr Lancaster says, 'break him to stand' or more generally to lie down, which is achieved by words of command 'Stay here' and the 'boss' or stop whistle. Complete obedience to this must be taught before the dog is put in with sheep.

Mr Capstick compared the dog's training, taking a long period of time, with going to school. Endless patience is required on the part of the farmer who must not persist too long and bore the dog, but must always make him obey. As Mr Lancaster says: 'Everything should be as natural learning at home in a field as on the moor.' It is bad policy to train a young dog alongside an old one; not only will it copy everything, including faults, but it will not learn to think for itself.

As the dog progresses he is taught to gather gently by approaching in a wide pear-shaped sweep so as not to upset the flock. This method is deployed in the outrun or 'fetch' of the trials. Gathering sheep is a dog's natural instinct and it is far more difficult to teach him to drive (take them away from his master). The dog must follow the whistle, not work on his own, and when driving never look back. To prevent this it is best not to drive straight but to cross-drive. When the dog is running blind, out of sight of his master, over a hill perhaps, then dog-sense comes in and the animal shows his true sagacity.

All the work that he does at the trials is the same as the every-day work on the farm only in a more acute form. Points at trials are awarded, amongst others, for the lift (how the dog gets up and approaches the sheep). One of the most difficult things is to shed correctly (singling one sheep from a flock). A sheep should be shed from the back not the front of the flock. At the pen a dog should be very steady. For trial work the handler's tone of voice, which must always be the same, is vital. If he is nervous at the stake (the stick where the farmer stands), the dog will

61. *Mr W. Hunter, Crow Trees, Swaledale, mucking with Dinah and a coup. Mr J. Hunter is scaling muck.*

MUCKING

62. *Mr Brian and Mr Francis Fawcett, Greenses, Swaledale, mucking with a low cart and scaling muck.*

69. Mr B. Fawcett, Greenses, near Keld, Swaledale, jagging bales of hay which have done away with the necessity of tying burdens.

MAKING A BURDEN

69. Mr B. Fawcett, Greenses, near Keld, Swaledale, jagging bales of hay which have done away with the necessity of tying burdens.

◁
63. Making a burden. Mr W. Hunter, Crow Trees, Swaledale, standing on a dess in the mew cutting a canch.

64. Laying out the burden rope. The rope up the wall has a loop at the end. Usually burdens were made in the mew and the loop was hooked over a nail on the back of the door.

65. Putting three canches on the rope where it crosses. To tie up the burden, the rope near the foot is lifted up and a very short length pushed double through the loop which is brought across from the wall side.

66. Tying the burden. A wisp of hay is put in the loop formed by the double loop, which is pulled tight first from the right and then from the front.

67. The loose end on the right in plate 64 is now brought up and taken under the central knot, pulled tight and tucked under the rope several times. A burden usually contains four to eight stones of hay, but can hold twelve. If carrying a large load, the horse would not be ridden.

68. With a burden slung on each side of Dinah, Mr Hunter sets off to the moor to fodder the sheep. Beaut is ready to follow.

MAKING A PAIR OF CREELS

70. *Mr W. Hunter, Crow Trees, Swaledale, begins making a pair of creels. The hazel branches, preferably straight and about 6 ft long, are cut green, bent and tied, and kept for a year or two. Tarred rope is first tied at the base of the hazel bows forming a square.*

71. *Rope is then tied to the top of the bow, and, knotted to the first ropes, is carried to the top of the second bow and tied. Cross ropes are then tied and knotted.*

72. *The finished creel, which should fold up flat. It is tied together at the top by a length of rope, by which it is hung on a nail in the barn.*

73. Mr J. *Alderson at Stone House, Keld, carrying a pair of creels. They hold two to three stones of loose hay and up to six stones when densely packed.*

74. *Stean sheep washing, Nidderdale (1908) showing the crowd of onlookers. On the left is a sheep which is half drowned.*

SHEEP WASHING

75. *The Wallbanks at Keasden Head wash hole (c. 1908). Note the wash folds and the dam formed of stones, sods and an old door.*

76. *Mr W. Calvert, Thorns, Swaledale, holding twins at lambing time. If you have an orphan lamb, you must make it drink from the sheep, and then when the milk has run through it, the ewe smells the turds and knows its lamb.*

77. *Mr C. Alderson, Black Howe, Swaledale. Following spaining, the tits of the ewes are being sealed off with plasters to prevent the gimmer lambs, which are returning to the heugh with their mothers, from sucking. Squares of strong brown paper, dipped on one side in hot pitch and tar, are pressed on with a wet sod.*

WORK AMONG THE SHEEP

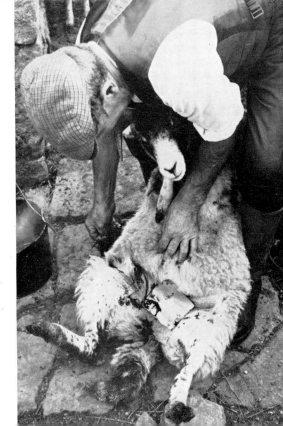

78. *Mr A. Dent and Mr C. Bowe horn-burning sheep on White Row Farm, Walden.*

HORN BURNING, SHEEP CLIPPING

79. *Mr G. B. Porter, Low Oxnop, Swaledale, clipping on a stool. He has begun at the front right shoulder and is working down the side, includ-*ing the belly, to the back legs and round the rump, clipping as far as possible to, or even over, the spine.

80. *The process repeated on* the other side. The tail has been clipped. (Boys learning to shear, began on tails.)

81. *The sheep turned over is nearly finished.*

83. Sheep-clipping on the Buttertubs Pass, Swaledale.

WRAPPING

82. *The sheep is turned the right way up with its legs dangling through the bars of the stool, the back is finished and the fleece drops off.*

84. *Mr G. B. Porter, Low Oxnop, Swaledale, wrapping wool. The fleece is laid down, outside uppermost. The sides are folded in, the fleece rolled up tightly and a length of neck wool drawn out, twisted into a rope, which is wound round the fleece, and the end tucked under.*

△

85. *Mr J. Wallbank, M Houses, Ribblesdale, dra the wool apart to make s dings for salving.*

86. *Taking a dab of salv the side of the finger from salving bowl fastened by handle to the greasing stoo.*

87. *Putting the salve on shedding.*

89. *Clipping on creels Riddings Farm, Howgill, S bergh (c. 1940).*

△
88. *The finger is then twisted over to press in the salve.*

▷
90. *The Bowdin family dipping sheep at Town Head Farm, Hebden, Wharfedale (c. 1910). The half barrel might have been used originally for mixing salve.*

SHEEP
SALVING,
SHEEP
CLIPPING
& DIPPING

91. *The Wallbanks and hired men salving sheep at Keasden Head (c. 1909).*

92. *Malham Sheep Fair* (c. *1910*). *The children in the foreground are all wearing clogs.*

SHEEP FAIRS

93. *Leyburn October Fair* (*1905*).

94. *Mr J. L. Peacock (1889–1967) with Nap and Lad and Swaledale sheep in Arkengarthdale.*

SHEEPDOGS

95. *Mr C. Alderson and Mac bringing sheep from the fell to folds for spaining on Black Howe Farm, Swaledale.*

96. *Mr Robert and Mr Thomas Rutter, Shoregill, Swaledale, milking on Gunnerside Pasture* (c. *1910*)

MILKING OUT OF DOORS

97. *Milking on Ellerlands Cow Pasture, Castle Bolton, Wensleydale* (c. *1900*).

98. *A farmer at Leyburn, Wensleydale, with budget or backcan used for carrying down the milk from cows on the pastures.*

99. *Donkey with backcans at Castle Bolton, Wensleydale.*

TRANSPORT OF MILK & BULL FAIR

100. *Hawes Fair in October (c. 1908), The bulls are fastened to a chain against the wall, top left.*

HORSE FAIR

101. *Brough Hill Fair: dealers bargaining for a horse* (c. *1938*).

GEESE

102. *Geese on Howgate, Askrigg, being driven down Wensleydale* (*1880s*).

103. *Geese at Settle* (*1907*).

know and become bewildered. When running doubles (two dogs together) each animal either answers to its own whistles, or the same ones are used prefixed by the dog's own name.

Breeders and trainers of dogs can teach the whistles to a new owner even over the telephone, but if one man is English and the other Welsh, for instance, then the intonation makes it almost impossible to learn the commands. It is feasible to change a good dog's whistles, but this might take as long as six months. On the other hand Mr Lancaster once gave his dog fresh whistles and perfected it in three evenings, and then won a doubles trial with it.

The eyes of a sheepdog are his greatest asset. He must be able to see quickly and to be able to eye (control) the sheep. It is possible to have too much 'eye', known as a hard eye, which means that the dog may be excellent when concentrating on a few sheep but cannot control a large flock. Dogs that eye early are not always the best in the end. Those that start at a year are often better. Unfortunately, sometimes a dog may work splendidly for a few years and then suddenly go right off.

Yet Maddie, Mr Lancaster's ten-year-old bitch, 'a great dog', had won seven trials before she was eighteen months old. 'She has it in her. Put her on the fell and away she goes, she's in her element.' Full of sheepdog lore, he told us the most difficult manœuvre to teach is to 'learn 'em to flank, to keep their distance from sheep and to go quietly. The quieter you and the dog are the better. Don't issue too many commands, and you yourself must have sheep sense'. Both Tom Lancaster and Laurie Peacock always found bitches more sensitive to commands than dogs, but on the whole dogs are more popular and many people consider them to be more even in their work than bitches.

Three gifts which are born in a dog cannot be taught. The first is to be able to recognize a wanted sheep and to single it out from a flock; the second is to be able to single out his owner's sheep from those of neighbours', which is useful, but can be awkward if you want to bring in strays; the third is to be able to set sheep buried in snow drifts, although an old dog, who could set, has been known to teach young ones. To do this the dog stands rigid on scenting the sheep.

Mr Lancaster had a wonderful dog called Fan who could set sheep. In one very bad storm he lost 203 sheep, but would have lost three or four hundred but for her. 'She set 'em', he said, 'thirty feet down; she was true as steel. She would walk on top of the drifts, all at once stop and *whinge* a little, and we would dig and find 'em.' Dogs cannot set dead sheep, which sometimes lie on top of live ones so that some may be missed.

For two periods of seven and eleven years Mr Thomas Joy was the shepherd in charge of 1,000 sheep on Grassington Moor. 'I had three good dogs—Lass, Lady and Scot. Lass was three years old before she was trained, and I never let her near the sheep for a month at first. She was always on the go *tittering* about, covering the moor twice over.'

In one of the storms of the winter of 1947 George Capstick, then managing his mother's farm in Howgill, started out with the farm servant at 9 a.m. on to the hill to gather. 'It takes a good man an hour to walk to the top of the fell.' They were returning with the flock in mist and snow, when suddenly the mist cleared and they saw four wethers. He loosed his dog, Ken, who set off to fetch them. Then the mist closed down again. They knew if they made enough noise that Ken would know where they were. But at the Fell Gate there was no Ken, and about 5.45 p.m. they returned to the farm to milk. At night he and his mother, who sat knitting 'with her knitting sheath and old bent needles', listened to the nine o'clock news. 'What do you say if we go up to the Fell Gate?' he asked. Looking over her spectacles, his mother replied: 'Yes, it's a good idea.' He and the man, taking a torch and lantern, set out. As they approached the Fell Gate they saw a sparkle. 'Them's sheep's eyes,' he cried, and there were the four wethers. Beside them deep in the snow, with a drift a foot high on his back, lay Ken. He could have left them and come home, but he hadn't. 'There's loyalty for you. I'm always thankful I went up to the Fell Gate.'

If there is real understanding between you and your dog, it will pull that last bit out to help you, but in the end of course it depends on the individual dog and on its pluck. So there they are: Ben, Bob, Laddie, Lassie, Fly, Hemp, Moss, Nell, Tiger, Toss, Wiley and all the rest of them, quietly going about their masters' business on moor and fell, day after day, year in, year out.

HORSES, CATTLE, PIGS, GEESE, HENS & BEES

ONCE the domain of the Cistercian abbeys and the yeomen of the dales, horse breeding as part of the economy of the farm has with a very few exceptions gone. It was never general in the West Riding dales, but in those of the North Riding, Tuke in *General View of Agriculture* (1794) writes: 'Horses constitute a considerable part of the stock of the high parts of the western Moorlands, the farmers there generally keep a few Scotch galloways, which they put to stallions of the country, and produce an hardy and very strong race in proportion to their size, which are chiefly sold into the manufacturing part of the West Riding and Lancashire, to be employed in ordinary purposes.' They were also in demand as pack-horses. William Howitt writing of Dent in *Rural Life of England* (1837) describes a race of dun ponies 'remarkably sure-footed and highly prized for drawing in ladies' pony-carriages'.

Tuke points to the origin of the Dales pony bred from the Scotch galloway. It is now a specific breed with a stud book beginning in 1917. In height 14.2 hands, compared with the 14 hands of its relation the Fell pony of Westmorland, it is still spoken of as a gallowa'.

Especially in the districts surrounding the horse fairs at Dent, Hawes and Brough Hill in Westmorland, the breeding and breaking in of horses were a part of farm life. At these and others, such as Skipton, Settle and Reeth Bartle Fairs, stallions, decked with ribbons, parading up and down, were a feature. Large numbers of *stags* (unbroken and unshod ponies) were rounded up from the fells for sale at the fairs for use in traps and commercial vehicles in towns. At Hawes about 1900 they fetched as little as £8 but usually £10 to £12.

'Our delight was breaking in horses. I've known us break in as many as four in one winter, work as well,' said Mr Hunter of Crow Trees, Swaledale. 'You 'ed ter mak a pun or two where you could,' remarked another farmer. And we have been told of a woman having time to break in a horse and still make a 4-lb. cheese every day. One method was to strap an old pair of trousers padded with straw to the stag's back. Or a breaking bit was put on; and kept in a garth, the animal *chiggled* (chewed) at the bit for a few days. Then long reins were attached. Mr R. B.

Spencer, the Hawes blacksmith, remembers stag-shoeing. About five animals were bunched close together in the shed. Then the smith, moving in, plated each of the two front feet first.

Mr R. Close (born 1882) living at Hazelgill Farm, Bowes, Teesdale, has suffered all his life, as he himself says, from 'horse fever'. There was always keen competition as to who had the best all-round galloway. 'I always had the fastest horse as we went to Barney Castle. I loved a horse as I do yet.' One year he wintered sixteen, and usually had three or four foals. When a young man, he asked to be halterer for 10s. for N. Bousfield at Brough Hill Fair. Bousfield replied that he could get a boy for 5s. But Close sticking to his price, said that if he didn't suit 1d. would do. Later he earned £1 and in time £2. A drove of up to 100 ponies might be driven to the fair by a horseman riding in front and others on foot following behind.

Once there they sorted them into Fell, pit and Dales, and when catching one in the different bunches, they had to hold on by the head or tail by main force. Later he took to climbing on the backs, going from one pony to another until he reached the one he wanted to halter. By the time they had finished, the ponies were half broken, and the buyers who had bargained for them in the old style by clapping hands at each bid, often rode them home (*see plate* 101). Stories abound of the long rides from many dales to Brough Hill, and of sometimes buying good-lookers which, next day after the dope had worn off, proved quite intractable.

An entry for 30th September 1871 in the day book of David Calvert, blacksmith of Gunnerside, reads: 'Me at Broughfill Bought gallow trash.'

Dales ponies, says Mr Close, must have a sweet head, nice shoulders laid back, short back, good loin, tail set well up, firm clean hocks and ankle joints, no white slash, no white above the ankles especially on the hind feet. There is an old saying, 'One white foot buy it/ Two white feet try it/ Three white feet go by it.' The colours are black, brown and grey. Formerly bred large for work on the farm, Dales ponies are now in demand for riding and to reduce the size a cross is being allowed with the Fell pony.

Although many were treasured, farm horses led hard lives. Mares often foaled in July, and had to work all hay-time pulling sledge loads up steep hillsides, then be cooled off for half-an-hour before it was safe for them to suckle their young. We have often been told of them plunging through snow drifts, falling into bogs (a horse with big feet had an advantage) or of their sagacity in avoiding bogs, or whilst grazing on the high pastures being struck by lightning.

Horses have almost gone from the farm but the keeping of cattle continues. Bulls of good quality were bought communally to improve the stock in the sixteenth and seventeenth centuries. When the eighteenth century surveys of agriculture were undertaken, in Craven and the upper parts of the dales the old long-horned breed prevailed intermixed with crosses with the short-horn kept at the lower extremities of the dales. The cross-breds weighed when fat 30 to 40 stones; and the dairy cows of Nidderdale of the mixed breed were described as 'both useful and handsome'. In the nineteenth century with the infusion of stock from the famous Bates and Booth herds of shorthorns, improvement was general. Noted breeders were W. Carr, Stackhouse, Ribblesdale, Francis Garth, Haverdale, Swaledale and the Willises at Carperby, Wensleydale.

Besides the native stock, many Scotch cattle were driven down from Scotland, especially to the cattle rearing district of the Craven highlands. Hurtley's description in his *Natural Curiosities of Malham in Craven* (1786) of the 5,000 cattle massed for sale in Great Close near Malham Tarn is famous. Here, beginning in 1745, the 'celebrated Craven grazier' Mr Birtwhistle, visiting the Hebrides and the northern-most parts of Scotland, had 20,000 head of cattle in this field in one summer 'every Herd enticed from their native soil and ushered into this fragrant pasture, by the Pipe of an *Highland Orpheus*'. 'There are now', says Hurtley, 'several other Graziers who go to the Highlands on the same business'; and indeed the trade continued.

For instance two families of Pratts in upper Wensleydale regularly visited Oban, Lanark, Stirling and the islands in the first half of the nineteenth century. A descendant, James Pratt (1852–1927) of Burtersett, stayed at the Caledonian Hotel, Lanark, for sixty consecutive years, visiting auction marts and farms to buy Scotch cattle, shorthorns and sheep. Lots of 40 to 100 cattle and any number of up to 600 sheep, walking fifteen to twenty miles a day depending on the weather, were brought down in September along the drove roads. The drovers came so far and then others took over. All slept wrapped in their plaids at night. Perhaps when they reached Haltwhistle, the dealer and his sons went to meet them, and then pasturing them on Wether Fell, Wensleydale, they sent the cattle off in droves to show at all the fairs, for instance at East Witton, Middleham, Hawes, Brough Hill, Gargrave and last of all Settle.[1] Mr E. Pratt still buys cattle in Scotland in spring and autumn. Now transported in cattle wagons by road, for many years until 1965 they were brought down by train.

When the Enclosure Acts of the late eighteenth and early nineteenth centuries were passed and the extensive cow pastures behind every village in the dales were allotted to individual owners and, divided into fields, were enclosed by walls, the system of cow-keeping was radically changed. At Redmire, Castle Bolton, and Preston-under-Scar in Wensleydale and at Gunnerside in Swaledale only partial enclosure took place.

The town pasture at Redmire, almost 300 acres in extent, has fifty-five gates, of

[1] Mrs A. N. Mason, Hawes, Wensleydale.

which one or two formerly went with every cottage or house in the village. There were three *byelawmen* to see that all was kept in order, and in the summer a herdsman brought the cows down to the standings, to which the cottagers carrying pails and backcans resorted. (It took a month to six weeks to train a heifer to stand still in the open.) A cow club, to which members subscribed and were paid its value if their cow died, was a communal form of insurance. Gradually the gates have been joined up, so that only four people, of whom only two having milking herds which they bring down to the farm buildings to milk, have cows.

At Castle Bolton, where they still employ a dogger-in who brings the cows down from Ellerlands Pasture, about ten people have milking cows, which they winter in the many small barns found in this area, mentioned in the chapter on farm buildings.

Change on the farm since the Second World War has also meant a reduction in the number of pigs kept for food. Killed and salted in November or December, they provided home-cured ham and bacon throughout the year. Bought from a dealer, who came round in a horse-drawn pig-cart or trap in early summer, they were fed on whey from the cheese making until the last few weeks of fattening on meal. A large household might have five to eight, and sell the hams. Pig-killing was an event, with the sudden influx of meat, the rendering down of lard, and the gifts to friends and neighbours. Parties, with games—dominoes and a form of hoop-la in Garsdale—often followed pig-killing. As it was said, every part of a pig was made use of except the whistle.

The keeping of geese also antedates the enclosures. Bred in Dent, Sedbergh, Garsdale, Swaledale, Mallerstang and Wensleydale, they were collected by dealers who drove them to Richmond or Darlington markets, making an average profit of 3d. to 6d. per head. Similarly from other dales they were driven to markets in the Vale of York, where they were bought by farmers to fatten on the stubble.

Driving was a tedious business requiring the utmost patience. To prevent their webs from splitting they were driven through pens containing tar and sand, often at the blacksmith's shop. The rate of travel of a drove of 100 to 200 geese was half a mile an hour, and they had to be rested for half an hour every mile. Seven miles a day was good going, and allowing a fourteen-hour day, from 4 a.m. to 6 p.m., it took six days to travel from Dent to Richmond. On the way geese which went lame might be sold off cheap. At Settle, where the geese were being driven down from the north, the men driving them wielded sticks with bladders tied at the end.[1]

It is often said that 'If it's a good lambing time, it's a bad goose hatch,' and up

[1] Recollections of James Dinsdale, Askrigg, Wensleydale (1843–1937) and Miss M. Procter, Settle.

to comparatively recently for those who afforded one, a goose not a turkey was the traditional Christmas dish. Even then it might be an old one boiled before roasting.

It is remembered that at Gayle and Appersett, Wensleydale, all the cottagers kept from four to six geese with a *steg* (gander) which lived on the green and by beck and river. Up to forty or fifty years ago it was usual to house the sitting geese in the kitchen, perhaps under the table or in a corner with a few stones round and a little bedding, or in a tea box, or under the dairy shelves. Some cottagers might have as many as five or six sitting. Each goose knew its own nest and walked in and out as it pleased. After hatching, and at about a month old, the goslings were sold to dealers for 2s. 9d. to 3s. in the 1920's. The proceeds paid a half-year's rent.[1]

Hens, described as 'pullan' in seventeenth-century inventories, were here as elsewhere traditionally kept by the farmer's wife for pin money, and mixed flocks of old and young birds were usual.

Although some bee-keeping continues, no one remembers the general keeping of bees for honey for sweetening. It appears to have died out over a hundred years ago. Tom Rawson, the estate ling thatcher at Swinton near Masham, made bee-hives of ling, which had the disadvantage of being somewhat heavy. The beeboles, square spaces let into garden walls, where the old-type straw or ling hives were housed, are to be seen here and there. Although beebole is the correct name, we have found them called 'holes'. Records were kept in diaries [2] of which bees in which hole had swarmed, usually in June, and stones of honey were collected. As elsewhere superstitions prevailed. When a member of the Holmes family of Gamsworth, Wharfedale, died over fifty years ago, the bees were put into mourning. It was thought that if they were not told, they would never do any more good.

[1] Mr A. Metcalfe and Mr T. and Miss E. Dinsdale, Appersett.
[2] The Garth diaries, Haverdale, Swaledale. (Entries in 1820's and 30's.)

CURES ON THE FARM

UNTIL comparatively recently in the more remote parts of the dales the cure of animal ailments was the province of the cow doctor or farmer, or in the case of horses' feet of the farrier, noted for their skills in healing. Although there were vets in lower Wensleydale, a qualified veterinary surgeon only came to live in the upper dale in 1948. Using medicines and salves whose recipes had been handed down for generations, the cow doctors were sometimes guided by printed works. In the last century Matthew and Thomas Mawer of Stean and Lofthouse, Nidderdale, possessed *The Improved Cattle Doctor* (1854), *Complete Cattle Doctor* and *The Farmer's Friend or Cattle Doctor*. Besides these *The Yorkshire Cattle Doctor and Farrier* by John Knowlson, first published in 1820, was widely circulated.

At a time when vaccines prevail, some elderly people remember that bleeding was practised by their fathers. For bleeding horses and cows a string or tape was tied round the neck so that the vein stood out. After making a hole in it with a pointed knife, the vein was opened with a *fleam* (bleeding knife) knocked with a light wooden *mell* (hammer). About half a lading can, nearly a quart, of blood might be drawn off. Bleeding is remembered as a remedy for a cow with sunstroke in Malhamdale. Quite recently in Swaledale a *blained* cow with bad eyes and puffy swellings was treated by taking an inch off the end of the tail to make it bleed.

As part of the equipment for doctoring horses, the old-time cow doctor or vet for that matter had a gag to keep the animal's jaws open, a balling gun with which to shoot in medicinal balls, and a horse twitch or *pirn*, which nipped the moustache part of the horse's upper lip and had the effect of quietening him (*see drawings on page* 59).

Nitre and turpentine were two familiar ingredients for horse cures and, a strong antiseptic, green salve or ointment (containing verdigris), was used for castration and by farriers for curing foot troubles. Entries in the day book of David Calvert, smith of Gunnerside, read: '1871 3rd May James Alderson Horse foot Bleeding at Home 6d., 22nd May Will Bell gallow[ay] foot dressing, Green ointment for it 6d., 18th June Will Rutter 2 new Shoes Shod with Lether and tar 6d.'

For giving liquid medicines the cow doctor or farmer used drenching horns, large ones perhaps made from the horns of Scotch cattle for cows, small ones for sheep, and fairly large ones for horses; but for the latter, as horses are more difficult to hold than cows, the pointed end was used and the wide end blocked up. Formerly remedies for cows consisted of powders mixed with water and treacle. When dosing a cow, the farmer held the drenching horn in the animal's mouth whilst a helper poured in the mixture from a jug. Care had to be taken to see that the beast was breathing at the right time or it might choke. It was regarded as a sin to forget to put the drenching horn back on its nail in the cowshed.

A general panacea adopted for the treatment of ailing cows was *rowelling* or *reulling* also called *pegging* or *seton*, recommended by the nineteenth-century books on cattle doctoring. The principle involved the insertion of an irritant under the skin 'to make the part laid open the seat of the disease'. Fifty years ago all milk cows, especially those in poor condition, were regularly rowelled; and one of the signs of an ailing cow with felon or hidebound was a tightness of the skin, usually quite loose.

One method, possibly the earliest, was to make a pocket in the skin of the chest of a cow immediately in front of the foreleg by cutting a slit about an inch long down to the rind, inserting a finger and opening out quite a large pouch between skin and flesh. Into this a few rolled-up leaves of setter-grass, tied up tightly with string, were inserted for twenty-four hours—no more. Setter-grass or felon-grass, *Helleborus foetidus*, is given as setter-wort in Bentham and Hooker's *British Flora*. Instead of it a piece of onion or a wad of cotton wool and coarse turpentine was sometimes used. Each day for a week a ball of lard and salt was put in to keep the opening, which festered, running. At the same time a bought felon drink was administered. The discharge was called *fay* in upper Ribblesdale.

A plant of setter-wort grows in the garden of Haverdale House, Swaledale, formerly the home of Francis Garth (1817–1911) a patriarchal yeoman greatly in demand for the doctoring of cattle. In the day book of Mr M. Clarkson of Reeth, veterinary surgeon, appears the entry among similar ones for 1902: 'Thos. Sunter, Spring End, Rowelling cattle at 4d. each 4s.'

In another method a rowelling or setter's needle, resembling a large packing needle, with a razor-sharp blade, was used. It either had a hole in the blade or a looped handle through which tape or string was threaded. The needle was jabbed into the dewlap, slanted downwards under the skin about three inches, and a length of tape with a knot at one end drawn through. Then a second knot was made at the other end and the two ends tied together. Each day the tape was pulled so that the wound remaining open festered, and 'all the evil humours were drawn out. The tape might be left in two years, by which time it had rotted away. Some were rowelled every year. They didn't know you'd done anything. If you had 'em all rowelled, the barn smelt terrible'. [1]

[1] Mr Gilbert Brown, Malham.

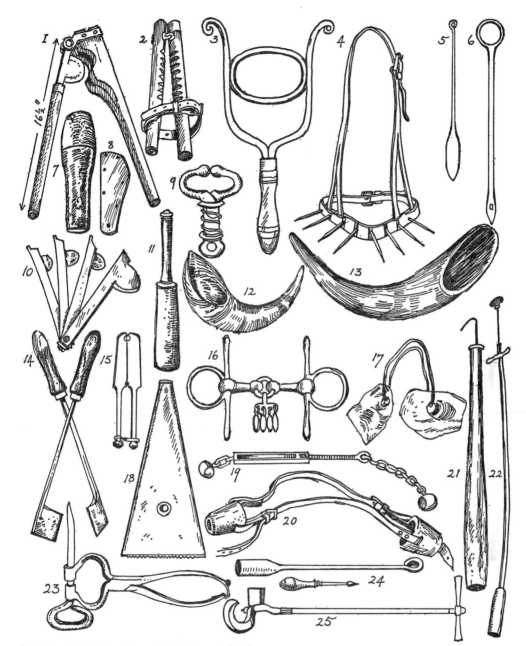

COW DOCTORS' APPLIANCES

1 Horse docking irons. 2 Pirning tool or twitch. 3 Horse gag. 4 Cow bridle to prevent sucking. 5 & 6 Rowelling needles. 7 & 8 Case and bleeding knife (fleam) with bone cover. 9 Bulldogs for cows. 10 Bleeding knife (fleam) open with brass cover. 11 Mell. 12 & 13 Horns for drenching cows and sheep, different sizes. 14 & 15 Gelding irons and clamp. 16 Breaking bit with four keys. 17 Rowelling stones. 18 Singeing iron for horses. 19 & 20 Horn trainers for cows. 21 & 22 Balling guns, wooden and iron, for horses. 23 Instrument for making hole for ring in bull's nose—made from sugar nippers. 24 Mazling iron and probe. 25 Steel tool for removing cows' teeth.

In Swaledale the 'reulling' needle (as it was pronounced in the dale) was used with a length of eight to nine inches of tarred string with a rolled-up leaf of setter-grass in the centre. When inserting the needle 'You had to be strong, it made the cow jump'. Two pieces of leather were threaded on at each end, held in place by a knot. The string remained in for about three weeks, during which time water ran out and matter collected. 'I've seen 'em run for a month.' [1] Instead of tape, twist (tobacco) or peeled *docken* root was used, or the string was smeared with coarse turpentine.[2]

Fragments of limestone with holes through them, rowelling stones, were some-times tied at the ends of the string. These holed stones may well have also served as witchstones, which were hung round a cow's neck or over doorways to ward off evil. Mr C. H. Lister has told us: 'When I was sixteen, I worked for a Mr Holden of East Woodhead, Wharfedale. There was a stone about the size of a golf ball, with a hole through it, hanging up in the stable. When I asked him what it was for, he said it kept the horses from dreaming.'

We were told in Nidderdale in 1966 that soil taken from under a hazel bush was given to cows—a cure recommended by Knowlson for a cow which had lost its cud. In the Muker district of Swaledale a sod was cut, turned upside down and given to calves with scour, and they ate it right down. Indeed, clean soil, rubbed fine in the palm of the hand, was eaten as a cure for heartburn in humans.

A certain cure for calves, aged up to half a year, with belly-ache, was to dose them with a tablespoonful of soot in a pint of scalded blue milk. Ringworm might be cured with an application of a mixture of bacon fat, flowers of sulphur and ordinary turpentine. To prevent them suckling or eating bedding or straw small tin pails with holes pierced in them were fastened to the calves' muzzles, as a cow was sometimes fitted with a leather bridle, with large iron spikes on the nose band, to prevent her sucking other cows' teats. Besides these there were horn trainers—a pair of either lead or leather caps joined by a buckled strap or an adjustable metal bar. The caps fitted each horn and could be tightened to pull the horns forward, as was the intention.

It was sometimes necessary to draw cows' teeth. 'You could tell they needed attention by the state of their coats. You need two men. One puts his arm round the cow's neck and holds its nostrils, whilst the other takes a special pair of pincers with the end at an angle and draws them out.' [3]

Mr M. Clarkson, journeying up and down Swaledale in a horse and trap, employed the common practice of applying a huge mustard plaster to a cow with

[1] Mr W. Hunter, Crow Trees, Swaledale.
[2] Mr J. R. Morphet, formerly of upper Ribblesdale.
[3] Mr G. Brown, Malham.

pneumonia. The paste of mustard and vinegar was plastered on both sides of the front of the ribs and over the shoulders, then covered with two or three pieces of brown paper, and 'sheeted up'.

Certain diseases afflict both sheep and cattle, for instance moss illness, which has the effect of making the animal fall down. The cure used to be to blow up the udder with a bicycle pump, tie the teat with tape, and leave it until the animal was relieved.

A skilled man was always in demand for the gelding of lambs. Formerly a clamp and red-hot gelding irons were used, and some farmers drew the testicles with their teeth. To our knowledge the stones, when fried, are still regarded by a few as a delicacy.

The greatest losses in sheep in the past, apart from those in winters like 1791, 1895 and 1947, resulted from braxy, which still for that matter occurs in this year's lambs in the late autumn, and is a stomach disease caused by a chill, resulting in a swelling which used to be cut with a knife and squeezed. Braxy is also used to describe the mutton of sheep which have died, not necessarily from the disease itself. This, as distinct from butcher's meat, was eaten in times of economic depression.

One of the strangest remedies, usually applied to hogs and six months' old lambs which appeared to be pining away, was *double scauping*.[1] Quite simply the frontal bone of the sheep's head was cracked by knocking it with the knuckle. This was done in the spring, allied with a change of pasture. Parasitic worms may have been the real trouble. Some say that it was the fresh pasture which did the good; others aver that you couldn't crack the skull of a fit sheep. One of these writers remembers helping with the operation in the 1940's.

Another ailment, sturdy, is now known to be caught by the sheep picking up a certain tapeworm in dogs and foxes. The affected animal, suffering from a cyst of young worm eggs and fluid on the brain, wanders round and round. Some men could judge the position of the cyst by the way the sheep turned or if an eye was affected. Sometimes a *mazling* iron, a bar with a hollow ring at the end, was heated and burnt through wool and skin or the place was cut, and then pressing with the broad end of a goose quill the sac was poked out. If this was not burst, the operation had been successful.

One of the characteristics of the true dalesman is the personal almost loving care and attention paid to the stock. Each sheep and each cow matter. 'What has she brought you?' is the question asked after a cow has calved.

[1] See *Folk Life*, vol. 5. 'Sheep "Scauping"', by M. L. Ryder.

PEAT

TURF, or peat, was for centuries, especially after the forests were cleared, the chief fuel used in the dales even where supplemented by coal from small local pits. Turbary, meaning the right to cut peat in a certain area or the area itself, occurs in grants to Yorkshire monasteries in the twelfth century. It is a common clause in deeds of property. When the Manor of Calton, in Craven, was sold in 1516, it included Malham Moor and a 'turbarye'. In village or hamlet each house which raised a reek had right of turbary on its own moor or common, and definite roads led to the peat bogs where the peat pits or pots were situated. Where rights did not exist 'turfegraste' was paid. This was collected from the inhabitants of Blean, near Semerwater, in the reign of Elizabeth I.[1]

Peat was used for smelting lead, for burning in lime kilns, and by blacksmiths for hooping wheels. Enormous quantities were cut for the smelting mills. In 1810 at Old Gang, Swaledale, there were twenty-two people 'Getting Peats' in loads, forty-two 'Peat Mewers', presumably stacking peats, and forty-seven 'Getters-up'. The first and second groups were men, but the third engaged in the drying process were mostly women. Not counting repairs to the peat stacks, thatched with ling, the cost of peat in that year was £337, admittedly considerably more than the £145 of the previous year.[2]

It is as a domestic fuel that it is now chiefly remembered. Most farmhouses formerly had a turf house. Peat was cut up to the Second World War at the heads of dales far from railways or small coal pits and on farms far from public roads. 'Many a farmer never saw coal,' we were told in Nidderdale, 'they couldn't have afforded it.' Peat is still cut by one or two people near Sedbergh, in upper Swaledale and on Grassington Moor, Wharfedale. As has often been said, 'It costs nowt but work'.

'Efter lambing time, yer started on at peeat,' says Mr J. Foster (born 1885), formerly of Beckermonds, Langstrothdale. 'It was a job to be done just like haymaking. Ivvery hamlet 'ed its own peeat pot i' them days—Oughtershaw on

[1] P.R.O. E 178/2627 Exch. Spec. Commissions, York. (1579/80)
[2] N. R. County Record Office. ZLB. A. D. Mills Account Book (1805–1885).

Nether Moss, Beggarmans and Dibdale on Dibdale Fell, Yockenwhit on Yocken-whit Moor, and Cray and Buckden on Carser.' 'Mi father was an expert peat cutter, and I followed him. I was a neat cutter,' affirms Thomas Joy of Grassington, Wharfedale.

There were both customary procedures and correct methods of working with special tools. On Grassington Moor the extensive peat pots, now filled with water, illustrate the first need—to provide adequate drainage. At these pots competition for a place was so keen that fights occasionally resulted, and to retain his own area a man had to work it each year or he forfeited the right to it. Here workmen dug their peats on Saturdays, farmers on weekdays, but never on Mondays, 'Skipton day' (market day).

The tools were formerly a cutter or flaying spade, a peat spade or slicer, and a *pricker*.[1] The cutter resembled a hay spade with a bent handle, or when a flaying spade was used (still remembered in Nidderdale) it was the original huge tool for taking off turfs when clearing the land. Both were used by pushing horizontally. The slicer had a small flange or wing, which enabled two sides of the peat, one broad and one narrow, to be cut at a stroke, and a broad-based wooden handle for casting peats into the barrow, for when wet they broke easily. It was used with a downwards action by the workman standing at the top of the face of the peat pot or sometimes with a horizontal action from the bottom (*see plates* 106–7). This tool made by the blacksmiths varied in pattern from dale to dale (*see drawings on page* 66). The pricker, a kind of hay spade, pricked or nicked the third side along the bottom of each spit or *bucket* (the latter word only heard in Nidderdale).

Some peat pots, or turf pits as they are called in the Bentham district, are deep, others shallow, depending on the depth of peat, so that the face or *bench* where the cutting proceeds varies in height from two or three spits to six, seven or more. First, old peat, which has been exposed to frost and is 'deead and neea good,' was cleared away, and the top layer of turf pared off. In Nidderdale they were cut as *flaughts* (sods) a yard long and 8 ins. to 10 ins. wide. By customary usage these were eventually replaced at the base of the face. Then the worker began with the slicer. A right-handed man worked from right to left, and the wing of the tool was on the right for him and on the left for a left-handed person to expedite casting. About six peats at a time might be supported on the spade and cast into the low peat barrow, which was placed close at hand at the appropriate side of the worker. Peat cuts like butter so that in general the strength of arms and shoulder sufficed without using the foot. Nor should tools need sharpening. John Close, a witness in a lawsuit of 1707, said that he used to dig peats for the vicar of Grinton,

[1] Described to us by Mr W. Ingleby, Nether Hesleden, Littondale, and Mr W. G. Wallbank, Keasden, who gives only the Down and Breast spades.

104. *Mr F. Whitwell and Mr F. Postlethwaite, Riddings Farm, Howgill, scything bracken for bedding. Rushes make better bedding than bracken, which stock inclines to eat, but bracken makes better manure* (c. 1940).

BRACKEN HARVEST

105. *Leading bracken for bedding on sledges on Riddings Farm, Howgill* (c. 1940).

106. *Mr J. Atkinson, West End, Lunds, Wensley-dale, cutting peat (1936).*

107. *Mr Waller Lancaster, Dowbiggin, Sedbergh, cutting peat, standing at the bottom of the peat pot.*

108. *Mr J. Atkinson leading peats in a coup from stacks. Peats are set up and drying in the foreground (1936).*

109. *The Wallbanks of High Grain, Eldroth, near Settle, setting peats into huts* (c. *1930*).

110. *The Wallbanks barrowing peats to the spreading ground* (c. *1930*). *The design of the barrow is unchanged since the Middle Ages.*

PEAT CUTTING

111. *Mr and Mrs Cherry Kearton and Martha cutting and spreading peats above Moor Close, Swaledale. They are using hay-spades instead of peat spades.*

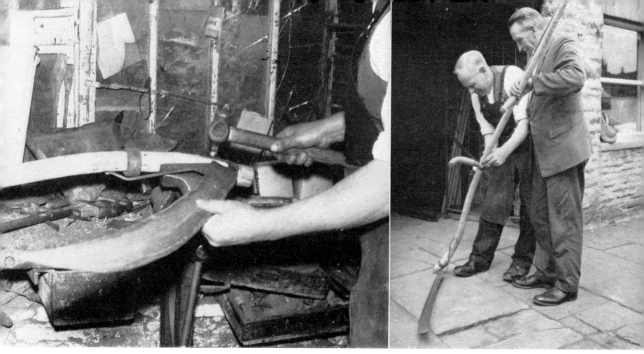

112. *Fitting up a scythe. Having roughly shaped a hollow in the pole, the blacksmith fits the red-hot heel of the blade into the kennel.*

113. *Mr R. B. Spencer and Mr F. Outhwaite Hawes Smithy, Wensleydale. The blacksmith adjust the lower nib, which should be the height of the hi when the pole rests on the ground*

116. *Scythemen, Grisedale. Mr Bell Pratt, Mr T. Lund and Mr G. H. Ashton*

114. *The upper nib is fixed an arm's length to finger tips above the lower.*

115. *The grass nail is in place. The blade should lie flat on the ground when held in a mowing position, and the tip be reached by the outstretched foot.*

SCYTHES & MOWING

117. *Mr W. Burton, his sons and a double horse mower, Snaizeholme.*

HAYMAKING   118. *The Daykin family, Newbiggin, Wensleydale, strewing.*

120. *Mr W. Calvert and Miss E. Calvert,*   121. *The foot is raised and hay drawn over it*
Thorns, upper Swaledale, making foot-cocks.   *with the rake.*

119. *The Postlethwaite family, Riddings, Howgill, turning hay in rows* (c. *1940*).

122. *Finally hay is drawn over again, making two thatches.*

123. *Making a jockey, which consists of two foot-cocks.*

HAYMAKING
MACHINES

124. *Mr J. Tennant, Cams-house, Askrigg, with a Bam-ford dasher, bought in 1916 for £10, converted to use with tractor in 1951, and discarded ten years later (c. 1950).*

125. *Mr William Hunter, Crow Trees, Swaledale, mak-ing windrows with a Jarmain swathe turner.*

126. *Mr Cherry Kearton, Moor Close, Swaledale, mak-ing windrows with a Nicholson International hayrake.*

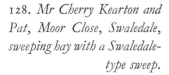

& SWEEPS

127. *Mr T. Harper, Dandragarth, strewing with a Nicholson strewer, bought new about 1952.*

128. *Mr Cherry Kearton and Pat, Moor Close, Swaledale, sweeping hay with a Swaledale-type sweep.*

129. *Mr W. E. Iceton, Blackton, Baldersdale, sweeping with a wing sweep. This was pulled by one or two horses. When drawn by two, the horses walked at either side of the windrow and as the load increased the wings opened wider.*

130. *Mr T. H. Alderson, Borwins, Wensleydale, and two Irishmen with a paddy sweep (Tumbling Tom) making pikes (c. 1948).*

PADDY SWEEP

131. *The driver has slightly lifted the sweep by the handles, so that the prongs dig into the ground, and as the horse continues forward, the sweep somersaults first on the prongs, then on the curved handles, leaving the load of hay behind it.*

LOADING A SLEDGE

132. *Mr A. and Mr W. Harper, Dandragarth, Garsdale, loading a sledge. A kemming is put on simultaneously at the outer corners of the sledge, which is pulled by the horse between windrows.*

133. *The rakes, held with teeth uppermost, run up kemmings, of which twenty-six (four layers of six and two on top) form a load.*

134. *Mr W. Metcalfe and Mr R. R. Heseltine, Askrigg, Wensleydale. The rope fastened to a lat of the sledge is drawn across the load on a rake's teeth.*

135. *Mr S. and Mr F. Woof and Blossom, Woodbridge Farm, Dent, pulling the rope tight over a sledge load of hay. A job for two people—one pulls round a lat of the sledge and the other ties a knot* (c. 1952).

TYING THE LOAD

136. *Mr and Mrs Jack Thwaite and Molly, Mouse Syke, Grisedale, leading hay with a sledge.*

HAYMAKING IN GRISEDALE

137. *The sledge load goes to the barn.*

138. *Mr W. Burton, Snaizeholme, Wensleydale, forking up. In the background his son is standing with a paddy sweep.*

139. *The hay is skilfully tossed with the pitch-fork into the forking hole.*

FINISHING THE HAY HARVEST

140. *Mr V. Wilkinson on Lowlands Farm Askrigg, Wensleydale, using a knag rake.*

141. *Mr J. Dixon Daykin and Mr Edgar Daykin demonstrate the making of a hay rope with a hay rake.*

142. *Chapman's wagonettes, Grassington, Wharfedale* (c. *1910*).

WAGONETTES AND CARRIERS' CARTS

143. *Carriers' carts, Richmond market-place, Swaledale* (c. *1908*).

144. *Public transport: char-à-banc, Kilnsey, Wharfedale (1927).*

CHARABANC & BUS

145. *The first bus in Wensleydale (1926).*

Swaledale, on Grinton Moor, but 'the place was inconvenient and spoilt his worketooles'.[1]

According to the width of spade and wing the size of the peats varied. They might be 8 ins. to 10 ins. wide by about 2 ins. thick and about a foot long. The expression 'a peat high', was once familiar. Peats cut for lead smelting, for Old Gang Mines, Swaledale, for instance, were about 2 ft. 6 ins. long. 'Ah wor just aboot height of a good mossy peeat/ And as small as a weasel to bewt': wrote Thomas Blackah, the lead-miner poet of Greenhow, in 'Me'y Cooarderoy Sute'.

Barrowed at once to the *liggin' grund* (firm dry ground) the peats were spread in close rows. Then in about a week's time or three days if it was good weather when they had hardened, they were set in *foots* (Baldersdale) or *footings* (Cautley). People went 'setting' or 'footing'. In this operation two, three or four peats, varying in number in different dales, were propped up against each other to allow the wind to blow through them. 'Peat and hay dry best wi' wind—sun kills, and May winds are better than June,' says Thomas Joy. In Wharfedale and Nidderdale they were next *hutted* or *hubbed* by heaping more peats round the original few with one laid on top. Whilst drying, they shrink considerably.

Finally they were stacked in a *pike*, rick or *ruckle* (Nidderdale) (*see plate* 108). The stacks were carefully made. A circle was marked out, and peats stood on end for the base. Built up with peats laid flat sloping downwards, leaving gaps between them, they tapered to a single one at the top. *Clots*, small broken pieces, were sometimes thrown inside. Once stacked they did not spoil, and could be led (carted) 'et efter' hay-time or even the following year. One stack amounted to one cart load. In a good summer people might harvest enough for two or three years.

Peat carts were of light construction and varied types. As pictured in Walker's *The Costume of Yorkshire* (1814), a Langstrothdale cart ran on solid wooden wheels; others were coups fitted with peat *hecks* (shelvings), or coups specially made for the job with high latted sides (*see drawing on page* 34). It is remembered that this peat coup, with a mat put in it, was used as a play pen for the Alderson children at Stone House, upper Swaledale, and that the children once climbed inside before a Sunday School anniversary and spoiled their best clothes with brown peat stains. 'And there weren't so many clothes then,' said Mrs J. Alderson.

In all these processes the children helped—spreading, setting and throwing the peats into the peat house. Farmers and farmers' sons often went peat cutting after milking until 9 p.m., or family parties, provided with food, journeyed to the peat pots for a day's work. 'If yer were cutting 'em yan efter anither, yer 'ed a few peeats bi yer got to t' end.'

Depending on how many fires were to be kept going and the size of cart

[1] P.R.O. E 134 Michs. 6 Anne No. 38 York.

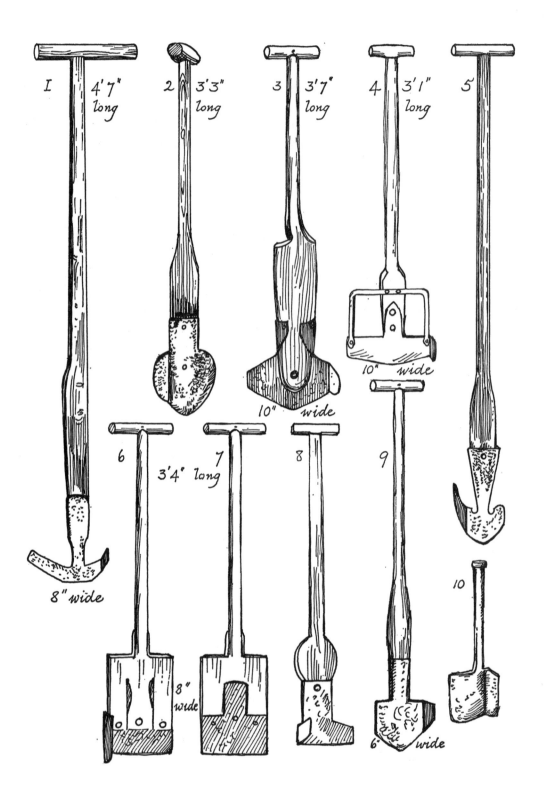

I   4' 7" long

2   3' 3" long

3   3' 7" long

4   3' 1" long

5

10" wide

10" wide

10" wide

6

7   3' 4" long

8

9

10

8" wide

8" wide

6" wide

(heaped up and often with sacks of peat piled on top), a farmer might lead fifty to a hundred loads. Some reckoned to burn a load a week on one fire. The top raggy peats which burnt away quickly were kept separate, for all was tidy in the peat house, and, used for lighting fires, 365 of these might be specially gathered. In Malhamdale a peat was buried under the fire range and next morning 'it were just seeame', and was employed for lighting the fire. 'We nivver used neea matches,' said Gilbert Brown of Malham. The peats from the bottom of the peat pot drying black and very hard compared favourably with coal and, burning better in small pieces, were broken on a wall top or on the knobs sometimes purposely provided at each end of the top of a fire grate. Peat burnt well with the small coal mined at Tan Hill pit up to the early 1930's. In Cotterdale, where West Pits supplied coal, some people burnt all-coal fires. But if they went out a burning peat was begged from a neighbour to re-light them.

Peat was brought into the house in skeps, scuttles, swills and *wiskets*, the latter made of plaited hazel near Slaidburn, in Bowland. Some farmhouses, as at Becker-monds, upper Wharfedale, had peat nooks, an alcove at the side of the fireplace where stood a kist for holding peats. 'Fetch me some *murls*' (crumbs and dust from the peat house floor), a mother might say to her child, if she required a hot fire to hasten the baking. 'You want some dry weather for peat. Ah've got manny a score carful,' an old peat-cutter said; and they were seldom prevented from harvesting their year's supply of fuel. 'It were warmer i' them days.'

PEAT SPADES

Specific types found in different dales. 1 Wensleydale. 2 Swaledale. 3 Nidderdale. 4 Upper Ribblesdale. 5 Early peat spade perhaps from Arkengarthdale. 6 Wharfedale (front view). 7 Wharfedale (back view). 8 Dowbiggin, near Sedbergh. 9 Baldersdale. 10 Baldersdale but not typical.

HAY-TIME

'IN the dales there is scarce an acre in tillage. Hay is the grand object of the farmer, and he bestows upon it the most sedulous attention, and has many difficulties to combat: the season commences late, the surrounding hills occasion frequent and sudden showers, and the meadows which are all natural abound with [herbs] . . . which being more succulent than the grasses properly so called, are more difficult to harvest than the produce of meadows where the grasses greatly predominate; yet, with all these difficulties, more hay is reaped in these dales with the same number of hands, than in any other place I have seen.'

The paragraph in *General View of Agriculture of the North Riding* (1794), written by William Fothergill at Carr End, near Semerwater, aptly describes dales' meadows and conditions. Only reseeded here and there and still abounding with herbs, neither the meadows nor the weather has altered. Good and bad hay-times are remembered for years. 'I ken being a month and nivver striking a *batt* [the forward sweep of the scythe],' is an all too familiar recollection of a wet time. Round Sedbergh a saying goes 'more rain, more rest'. And another from upper Nidderdale states, 'They'd rather see the devil come out of t' hills than a cartload o' peat before hay-time,' meaning that the good weather has come too soon.

The processes of winning hay fall into three groups—mowing, haymaking and leading. Although mowing machines were being made in Ripon in the late 1850's, they were not introduced into the dales for some time. It is recorded in the diary of Francis Garth, Swaledale, in 1862 that he bought one of Wood's Patent Mowers for £20. At about the same time John Whitel (1846–1928), Low Oxnop, Swaledale, tried out a machine in a meadow on the roadside. 'People came for miles to see it. It was like a fair.' [1] 'I remember the first mowing machine in Grisedale; it would be about 1895.' [2] The early heavy machines were not approved. It was thought that they spoilt the fog, and the different action of cutting did in fact slightly delay growth. Nor at first did they much affect the staff employed. Francis Garth still went on hiring twenty to thirty men and women.

[1] Mrs M. Waggett b. 1887 at Low Oxnop, Swaledale.
[2] Mrs T. Harper, Dandragarth, Garsdale.

Hand mowing is nowadays only remembered by the very elderly. 'Mi father was a grand mower; he'd been browt up wi' it,' they say. The poles and blades of the leas (scythes) were a different pattern from those of the present day. The long almost straight shafts, the Kendal poles, made of willow for lightness, had a slight cast near the base. Sometimes people made their own. They were supplied whole-sale over a wide area by the Hodgsons, blacksmiths of Dent, or bought from iron-mongers, such as Spence's of Richmond and Manby's of Skipton and fitted up by the blacksmiths. We obtained one in 1965 from the Hawes smith, the last he said he would have.

The blades, which 'came up to the chin', were at most 5 ft. 6 ins. long and 3 ins. wide and were forged in a solid piece, not with a welded base as later. Made of softer steel than nowadays, if a stone was hit the blade bent rather than broke.

Before hay-time, men sorted through a pile of poles at the smithies to find one which they fancied, and setting up the lea with pole, blade, *nibs*, heel hoop, wedges and grass nail, to suit the individual scythemen was 'a terrible carry-on' (*see drawing on page* 71 *and plates* 113–15). When properly set up, the lea should balance on one finger held under the lower nib. The saying 'as twined as a grass nail' originates in the twist in the nail as it joins blade to pole, and the triangle formed by it and the pole supported the cut grass and carried it neatly into the swathe.

Attached to the top end of the pole by an iron ring and pike (pin) was a square wooden strickle for whetting, usually made of unseasoned oak. To prepare it an iron strickle pricker was hammered on all four sides to make small *delfs* (holes), often a boy's job, so that either tar, tallow or grease spread on with a stick *clagged* to—not much or it would melt on a warm day. Sometimes a piece of fat bacon was rubbed on. Sharp sand was then thickly added. Lea or tarn sand could be bought, or was made by hammering a piece of coarse sandstone with a bukker (flat iron hammer), but it has also been collected from the shores of every tarn in the dales for this purpose, brought back in bags after shepherding or fetched in June on a special outing—enough for the year. One farmer, whose source of supply was Fountains Fell tarn, said: 'If they got tired bringing it home, they let a bit out.'

Sand was carried in the hay field in the Keasden district near Settle in a cloth pouch shaped like a postman's wallet, and was shaken out for use on to the flap. Elsewhere it was held in the hand, and the sides of the strickle were one by one pressed down on to the sand, which was flattened down with a knife. Sometimes it was carried in a can or round bottle with which it was rolled firmly down on the strickle. Grease horns appear to have existed in the dales in the distant past. Only the two opposite sides of a strickle are used when whetting; but if the four sides

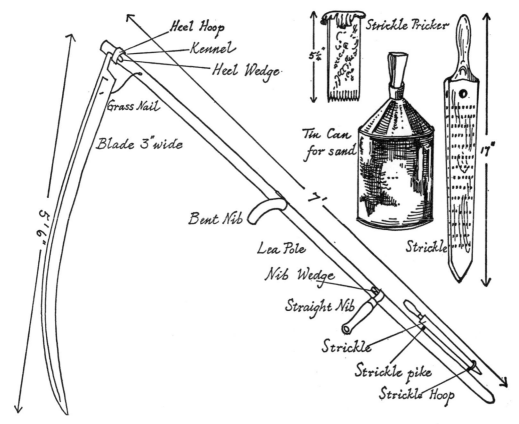

Heel Hoop
Kennel
Heel Wedge
Grass Nail
Blade 3" wide
5' 6"
Bent Nib
Lea Pole
Nib Wedge
Straight Nib
Strickle
Strickle pike
Strickle Hoop

Strickle Pricker
5½"
Tin Can for sand
17"
Strickle
7'

SCYTHE AND STRICKLE

were sanded properly, the strickle lasted all day or longer; opinion varies. Rain spoilt it and a cloth to dry it was often carried. The strickle was essential to the balance of a lea, and if it dropped off the scytheman knew at once.

Chiefly because every man sharpened his differently, it was an unwritten law that a man's scythe was his own and that no one else should use it. Whetting was the secret. A good scytheman was a good whetter; he put on a long edge from the heel to the tip of the blade. 'If you couldn't whet, it took your guts out.' 'Thou wasn't annywhere unless thou could cut t' hairs off thi leg. They thowt as much about their scythes as we do about pocket knives. They wadn't leave 'em even at dinner time and at the end of hay-time they dried and greased 'em.'[1]

Many hired men, both Irishmen and others, brought their scythes with them. The former travelled by rail. Once there was an accident in which several people were killed and the scythes in the guard's van badly damaged. For the Irishmen

[1] Mr J. Graham (b. 1880), Nidderdale.

the disaster lay not so much in the loss of lives but in the harm done to their scythes.[1]

Formerly an acre, so-called although it was slightly less than the statute acre, was regarded as equivalent to a day's mowing.[2] 'I could mow an acre reg'lar away.' It was within any man's capacity, but we also hear 'there's a difference i' men'. One could mow two acres a day without getting up especially early. Others recall feats of three in one day, and of six acres in two days. Mowing always began early in the morning. They were wakened at two or three o'clock. 'There wasn't mich bed for yer then.' [3] 'You should mow on a darkly day, starting about four while the dew is still on the grass. You can't mow in the hot sun. It's far too hot.' [4] 'Yer took scythe off t'tree when yer could hardly see to whet.' [5]

In a field full of mowers the leadsman or foreman, the best mower, led the others in an echelon formation across a field. A scytheman was able to cut a breadth of eleven to thirteen feet and strike a batt of three feet, some say a breadth of seven or nine feet and a one or two foot batt. They mowed one way across the field and then walked back to begin again in order that the swathes fell in the same direction. 'Mi father could mow so smooth, there were no ribs in it. His batts were dead on.' [6] Most scythemen prided themselves on carrying the grass at one strike into the swathe and not having to lift it to one side with the tip of the blade, known as 'grassing-off'. 'I could mow at seventeen as well as onny man. There used to be hay right down to t'watter fra High Greenfield to Beckermonds. To keep t' midges off, we covered our faces wi' butter muslin.' [7]

At Low Oxnop, Swaledale, they always hired the same three Irishmen, brothers, who had come for thirty years and their father and uncles before them. They were up at 5 a.m. and before they went out had a big jug of milk and bread and cheese. They expected breakfast at eight o'clock, and became edgy if it was late. These three were thought of as the best mowers who came into the dale. It was a sight seeing them as they all struck alike and began just so far the one behind the other, with the oldest in front. They may have counted the strikings, because they always started and stopped at the same time.[8]

Twelve men are remembered mowing in the big meadow at Longridge, Bishopdale. At Keasden near Settle we were told of W. R. Wallbank leading a field of ten

[1] Mr W. G. Wallbank, Keasden.
[2] P.R.O. E 178/4801.
[3] Mr A. Ashton (1866–1956), Lunds, Wensleydale.
[4] Mr W. Bayne, East Cowgill, Dent.
[5] Mr R. H. Lambert, Knight Farm, Little Stainforth, Ribblesdale.
[6] Mr F. Graham, Grimes Gill, Healey.
[7] Mr J. Foster, formerly of Beckermonds, Wharfedale.
[8] Mrs M. Waggett, Low Oxnop, Swaledale.

men at a fast rate when his scythe blade struck a stone and broke in half. The others threw their caps in the air and shouted with glee. From 1897 to 1903 Mr Ernest Campbell mowed the sixteen acres at Cosh, Littondale by himself. Jeremiah Metcalfe of Oldcotes, Littondale, had eighty acres to mow alone. Starting at 4 a.m. each day he went on rain or shine, never stopping until all was down, and getting in the hay in between. In upper Wensleydale they sometimes tied old gig umbrellas on to themselves to protect their backs if it was raining. 'You had to get it down.'[1]

In several parts of the West Riding dales fields are named Dearbought, for which the explanation, always the same, is that a man killed himself mowing for a wager to gain possession of the field. Another legendary story relates how a mower declared that he had found a silver guinea; but it turned out to be a piece of a crowbar which he had sliced off with his scythe. Others challenged their men to cut in half at one blow an upended wrapped-up fleece.

Before Irishmen started coming, all sorts of men used to be hired for haymaking —fishermen, quarrymen, even blacksmiths whose work temporarily ceased during the season. 'We had five big bedrooms at Keasden Head, and often hired ten men.'[2] Some workers were hired out of Westmorland or Cumberland, whence they walked. As far as can be judged, Irishmen have come to the dales for hay-time for well over a hundred years, and were hired at local markets or at June Fairs such as those at Bentham and Skipton. They often went to the same farm year after year, and were sometimes housed in the bedrooms of ruinous houses with which the dales formerly abounded.

In the old days of a hundred or more years ago gin was the hay-time drink obtained from local breweries or the inns. But latterly beer was usual, and a barrel was bought in beforehand. 'If you had an Irishman and didn't get out the beer, he'd be saying "I'm walking down t' road" meaning going to seek work at the next farm.'[3] Once a farmer at Nether Hesleden, Littondale, who owned three other farms, hired thirteen Irishmen and bought in thirteen barrels of beer. It was such a bad hay-time that the work he got out of them didn't pay for the beer they drank. People also remember drinking botanic beer and warm oatmeal water which prevented chills on the stomach.

Wages for a month's work were at the turn of the century £5 for a month. £6 was considered almost over generous. After the Second World War this sum reached £35 to £40 a month, rose to £60 in 1953 and is now likely to be £75. But with the introduction of many machines few men are now hired.

[1] Mr J. Dixon Daykin, Askrigg, Wensleydale.
[2] Mr W. G. Wallbank, Keasden.
[3] Mr W. Calvert, Thorns, Swaledale.

The sequence of the processes [1] of haymaking—strewing, turning, making foot-cocks and windrowing—was always followed and held good up to the gradual introduction of hay-time machinery drawn by horses towards the end of the last and the beginning of the present century. They have only faded out since tractors replaced horses in the last twenty years. In some cases they are still practised.

Latterly foot-cocks were not part of usual haymaking routine, except in poor weather (see plates 120–3). In the bad summer of 1965 thousands and thousands were made all over the dales. We are told: 'The old folks wouldn't have thought they'd made hay properly if they didn't make foot-cocks.' [2] 'We would put it in foot-cocks and *jockeys* (larger cocks) two or three times and shake it out by hand. When shaken by hand, it parted and broke up better.' [3] In former centuries cocks had a use other than drying the grass, for when tithe hay was collected in kind, one cock in ten was taken. They were called *lapcocks* in Nidderdale and the jockeys were *hubs* and *hobs* in the West Riding dales.

Forks, referred to by William Fothergill as 'the miserable invention of idleness', were not as much used as rakes within recollection. Even rakes were not approved. 'When we were lads, we were nivver allowed to use rakes.' [4] Up to fifty or sixty years ago *straw* girls or *straw* boys [5] about four to a mower followed the scythemen across the field strewing the grass by bending low and tossing it alternately with each hand over the opposite shoulder. In this way the hay was not trodden underfoot and lay as 'light as possible'. The paddies (Irishmen) using forks, could *scale* (strew) two rows at a time of the heavy thick hand-mown swathes. [6]

Until recently to make large cocks, called *pikes*, was usual practice. They were carefully built to turn water and combed down the sides with a rake. An almost forgotten art was making a hay rope to throw over the pike to protect it in winds. For although haymaking takes place in July, winds, sometimes small whirlwinds, can play havoc. A *thraw-crook* or a rake was used to make ropes. Either implement required two people—hay was drawn out of the bottom of the pike, and a loop made to fasten round the thraw-crook or round the teeth of the rake. Then a lad winding his thraw-crook or rapidly twisting a rake moved backwards as the rope lengthened and as the other worker fed the rope with hay from the pike. When finished it was either tied in a loop or with string, and was weighted down with stones at the other side of the pike (see plate 141).

[1] See *General View of Agriculture in the North Riding* (1794), p. 49–51.
[2] Mr W. Calvert, Thorns, Swaledale.
[3] Mrs W. Waggett, Low Oxnop, Swaledale.
[4] Mr T. Kirkbride, Askrigg, Wensleydale.
[5] Mr R. Jackson, Horton-in-Ribblesdale, and others.
[6] Mr W. Bayne, East Cowgill, Dent.

Up to the Second World War many a dales' farmer managed his hay-time with one or two horses and a staff of four or five depending on the size of the farm, a mowing machine, hay rake, strewer, and sometimes but by no means always a swathe turner, all pulled by a horse, and the two latter driven by the wheels of the machines as they rode along the ground. Other helpers or relations might come along at night.

In the final stage before 'leading', the making of windrows, two people working side by side raked as far as they could comfortably reach, and drew the hay into a windrow by overlapping one side a little over the other. To make windrows for jockeys you only draw the hay together.

When hay is really dry, having had the sun on it and been made right, it is crisp and blue. 'My father would have it dry. It had to be dry': the elderly people aver. Bad hay spoilt by rain is said to be red, and when altogether beyond hope is *rated*.

Next the dry hay had to be carried to the barn, usually situated in the meadow itself or in the next—seldom very far away. For this sweeps and sledges were used. A farm had one sweep, but might have two or more sledges. Arthur Young in *Tour Through the North of England* (1771) depicts a hay sweep, evidently uncommon, which he calls a machine. Resembling the back of a wing sweep, it had two curved beams joined by six uprights, and was drawn by two horses. The different patterns used latterly in the different dales are shown on page 77. In *General View of Agriculture* a hay sledge is illustrated which resembles the Swaledale sweep. Sometimes sweeps were home-made, but were more often ordered from the village joiner. Failing one, a gate was used. Most were tipped to unload them on arrival under the forking-hole of the barn (*see plates* 128–31).

Sledges pulled by one horse varied slightly from dale to dale in the angle of the rake. The correct method of loading required three people, two to load and one to lead or ride the horse (*see plates* 132–5). Sometimes the jockey, a boy or a girl, was the farmer's child but might be hired specially for the job. The sledge was pulled between two windrows, and two men at each side, holding their rakes upside down, set about *running heaps*, and not lifting the rakes from the ground each gathered together a *kemming* (an armful literally meaning a combing). Carrying it between arm and rake, they placed it upended on two corners of the sledge, then repeated the process for the other two corners, and filled up the centre with two more placed flat. For the second layer kemmings were placed across the corners, again with two in the middle. A ten-foot sledge holds twenty-six kemmings in four layers of six with two to bind the load placed on top. Mr T. Harper of Garsdale has described the method, which in other dales differs slightly. Some say three layers with three on top; and kemming is a word largely forgotten. A rope, tied to a hole in the back bar of the sledge, was thrown over the load or carried over it with a rake and then pulled tight round a *nog* (peg) at the front. On the steep slopes of Swaledale it was usual to tie at the front if you were going uphill and behind if you were leading downhill.

'When it got to t' forking-hole it was reet.' Sledge loads were tipped off sideways. Then the forker-up had to toss the hay with a pitchfork through the hole and into the mew, where a perspiring man or woman spread it evenly and trod it well down.

If the work had not already been fitted in, the grass on the borders of the fields under the walls, where the mowing machine could not reach, was mown by hand, called *piking* in Wensleydale and *hacking* in Swaledale.

Last of all *knag*- or drag-rakes, called *rovers* in Keasden, were pulled by hand up and down the meadows to collect into small rows every wisp of hay which had been missed. Henry Best's *Farming and Account Books* (1641) has a paragraph on 'Trailinge of the Sweathrake' used in his case after the corn harvest. In the *Wensleydale Advertiser* (30th June 1841) is an advertisement for 'Holyoak's Patent Leicestershire Drag Rake'. These implements are so designed that they ride on curved iron teeth, varying in number from twenty-six to thirty-four. They were dragged across where the windrows had been made, because that way the hay is more evenly scattered over the field and more easily raked up. When four or five people were drag-raking, it was helpful to be ambidextrous, for when all turned round to work back up the field they could change hands and see better where to follow. Drag-rakes are on occasion still used (*see plate* 140).

The old methods with their exacting endeavour were further eroded by the tractors which both power and pull the new haymaking machinery. The baler, introduced during the early 1960's, and more recently elevators to carry the bales up to the forking-holes, have largely done away with sweeps, sledges, windrowing, and forking-up. Yet however good the mechanical aids, sun and wind are essential.

A great deal of fun has gone out of haymaking. 'Aren't yer feet tickling?' may still be asked as the end of June draws near and farmers' families are ready to start. At times many a household never went to bed at all, and in wet weather work still has to be done over and over again. But in a fine year the meadows with a good staff of workers were cheerful places. Everyone had their own job. There were and still are favourite fields often with wonderful views. *Drinkings* were occasions for rest, sustenance for further work and the telling of tales. No one now will ever call their ten o'clocks *donfron*, the old Swaledale word, but perhaps they will look up and say, 'If there's enough blue sky to make a pair of trousers it's a hay day.'

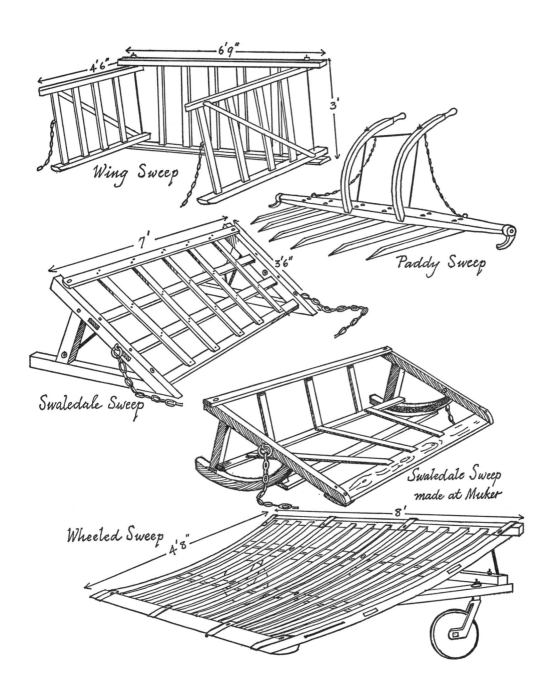

Wing Sweep

Paddy Sweep

Swaledale Sweep

Swaledale Sweep
made at Muker

Wheeled Sweep

HAY SWEEPS

'We've mown off' is still said when all the fields are mown. Those who finished first went, as some still do, to help those who had fewer resources or who on account of the altitude of their farms had a late hay harvest. 'Hay in the barn is the same as money in the bank' is a realistic saying. Last of all the *mell*, supper with perhaps a potato pie or meat and cakes, sometimes followed by games, marked the end of the annual ritual and effort.

JOINERS, CABINET MAKERS,
WHEELWRIGHTS & RAKE MAKERS

WHILST the local cooper, wheelwright and cabinet maker have gone, a joiner still has a workshop in many villages. In it old tools, their prototypes going back to the Middle Ages and even to antiquity, may still be seen—the axes, drawknives, *wommels* (augers), gauges, bradawls, adzes of different types, complicated moulding planes and even the huge obsolete pit and framed saws.

Village joiners combined all branches of woodcraft. Most had a constructional manual such as *Nicholson's Guide to Carpentry, General Framing and Joinery*, and cabinet-makers were guided by specific prices for every part of a piece of furniture as printed for instance in *The Preston Cabinet- and Chair-makers Book of Prices Agreed upon July 1802* which belonged to Thomas Brumfitt of Skipton. Work sent them all far afield. They took the mail coach from Skipton to Buckden, Wharfedale, or walked from Leyburn up into Coverdale or they struggled up steep hills from Askrigg, Wensleydale, with horses and carts, to help build houses in Swaledale.

In villages and market-towns alike businesses passed down from father to son. In Wensleydale the Thompsons were joiners at Bainbridge and Askrigg from the end of the seventeenth century until the middle of the nineteenth and at Leyburn the Winsbys, joiners, cabinet makers and wheelwrights, go back to the early eighteenth century. At Burnsall in Wharfedale the Clarks' business was founded by Richard Clark in the 1840's, and latterly three brothers served the village as blacksmith, wheelwright and joiner, all on the same and still existing premises. The Brumfitts at Skipton and the Calverts at Gunnerside, Swaledale have been cabinet makers since the eighteenth century. Normans and Parkinsons of Richmond, now defunct, have left behind well-made Victorian furniture, labelled with their names. A Parkinson advertisement of 1890 offers mahogany chairs with hair seating for 10s. 6d. and drawing-room suites in walnut with embossed Utrecht velvet for £7 15s. to £8 10s.

Generation after generation served their time, that is, were apprenticed, sometimes to a relative, sometimes to a stranger many miles away. In 1830 Thomas Winsby went to Skipton to Edward Brumfitt, his son John went to Varvill's at

York, probably the well-known firm of plane-makers, and Thomas's great-grandson, the present Mr John Winsby, was apprenticed at the age of fourteen to his grandfather, John Winsby of Leyburn, who used to say: 'Perfection, lad, perfection, but you'll never attain it', or to the apprentices in general, 'You wood-spoilers'. When he started work after his apprenticeship Mr Winsby earned 6½d. per hour. Thomas Weatherald, grandfather of Mr M. Weatherald of Askrigg, Wensleydale, served his time in London, coming home for holidays with a carpet bag slung over his shoulder. All speak of the special skills of the old craftsmen and of the constant practice which made work almost automatic.

Every joiner's shop used to have a saw-pit, in which tree-trunks were sawn into planks with the pit-saw and converted into boards with the framed saw. The pit-steadings have been filled in except at the joiner's shop at Kettlewell, Wharfedale, where one measures 40 ft. by 8 ft. wide by 5 ft. deep. Logs were rolled on or winched into position and made fast by wedges and chains. The top and bottom sawyers then started their tedious day's work. The top man who was in control marked the tree by snapping a taut line rubbed with chalk along the length of the log and also decided when to stop and oil or sharpen the saw. The man in the bottom, the pit sawyer, pulled the saw down. The pitch of the blade could be altered to suit the height of a man.

Journeymen, specializing in the work, went round from place to place. 'To 2 men sagin [sawing]' at 7s. a day for eleven days is recorded in a Winsby ledger of November 1810. When working for wages at Leyburn, the men used to chant to the rhythm of the sawing, 'Addle and tak 't. Addle and tak' t' (earn and take it); but when on piece work they changed to, 'Mean t' ev 't. Mean t' ev 't' (mean to have it).

The monotony of the job induced sleep. Mr P. Calvert of Gunnerside remembers when he was a boy working in the pit that his father or uncle gave the saw a jerk if they thought he was slacking off. Mr W. Bayne, Cowgill, Dent, recalls seeing his father and mother working at the saw-pit at the Weaving Sheds, Cowgill. His father directed operations from the top, whilst his mother, covered in saw-dust, was below in the pit-steading. It is not the only record of a woman working as the bottom sawyer.

Examining some of the old ledgers which have been kept, the reader is struck by the amount of repair work, which only brought in pence—the bread-and-butter work of the trade—supplemented by the regular making of farm tools and household utensils. In a Clark account book dating from the 1840's anything is repaired from a chair to a crutch. At the other extreme, when chapel, school, church or poorhouse was built, it was a red-letter day for the village joiner. The ledgers are also a mine of dialect words and contain wonderful examples of phonetic spelling.

146. *Shandry, a cart on springs, Askrigg, Wensleydale (1880s).*

SHANDRY & TRAP

147. *Mr Harry Robinson, the postman at Buckden, Wharfedale, delivering the mail at Deepdale, Langstrothdale (1926).*

148. *Mr B. Alderson, Gayle Mill, Wensleydale, with two framed saws.*

149. *Mr Norman Clark, Burnsall, Wharfedale.*

150. *Mr T. and Mr B. Alderson, Gayle Mill, with a pit saw.*

151. *Mr S. Brumfitt, Skipton, with files for carving, dies and ledgers.*

152. *Mr John Winsby, Leyburn, Wensleydale, in his workshop.*

153. *Curled elm watch case made by Thomas Winsby in 1837. He made three as souvenirs from the old elm in Leyburn market-place. They cost £3 5s. each.*

JOINERS & CABINET-MAKERS

154. *Mr W. T. Thompson chiselling mortices in the naf (hub) for the spokes; the position of the twelve holes has been marked out by dividers and two holes made by the brace and bit.*

155. *Measuring with the spoke set gauge to give the dish of the wheel. The gauge has previously been fixed to the centre of the naf by a large screw.*

158. *Using a gauge to judge how much to take off the tip of the spoke to correct the dish or the felloe would not be plumb.*

159. *Shaping the spokes by eye with draw knife. A spokeshave, plane and scraper are also used.*

156. *Mr W. T. Thompson and Mr R. J. Heseltine hammering in the spokes.*

157. *The wheel is now placed on a wheel stool and with a tramel the spokes are measured for the correct length, 19 in.*

WHEELWRIGHT MAKING A CARTWHEEL

160. *After sawing the tenons on the spoke ends, marking where the spokes will fit in the felloes, which then have holes bored in them with the auger.*

161. *Drawing the spokes together to fit the felloes. Note dowels between these. The inner side of the felloes has already been shaped. All is hammered tight and planed off.*

162. *Mr R. Haygarth, Dent, sitting on a horse, making rake teeth knocked through a cast steel moulder with a mallet. Only 500 to 600 can be made in an hour. They fall through into a box below.*

163. *Rounding the shaft.*

164. *Snipping teeth ends. This must be done on both sides, the head being moved along for each tooth and then turned over. Note bows in a rack on the right.*

165. *Boring holes in rake-heads.*

166. *Knocking the rake together. The bow is in the vice. To secure the parts, tiny wooden pegs are driven in where the bow fits into the shaft and where the bow and shaft fit into the head.*

MAKING HAYRAKES

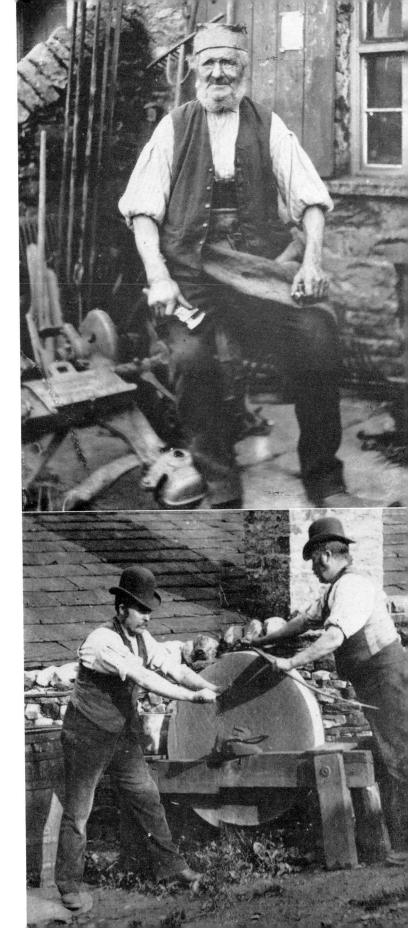

167. *David Calvert (1819–1906), black-smith at Gunnerside, Swaledale. He is sitting on a mowing maching and wearing a paper hat.*

BLACKSMITHS

168. *William and David Calvert, sons of the above David, sharpening a scythe and wearing bowlers, at Askrigg, Wensleydale, in the 1880s.*

169. *Measuring the circumference of a wheel with the traveller. Mr J. H. Tallon and Mr J. J. Tallon, senior, at Barbon smithy.*

170. *Measuring the inside circumference of the hoop starting at a chalk mark on both the hoop and the traveller and counting the number of rotations.*

173. *Carrying the red-hot hoop, which has been heated in a circle of burning logs for about three-quarters of an hour, to place on the wheel, screwed down on the tiring platform.*

171. *Heating the hoop for piecing.*

172. *Piecing the hoop.*

BLACKSMITHS HOOPING A WHEEL

174. *Slaking the hoop so that it contracts and tightens.*

175. *Having hammered the hoop down on one side, the smiths turn the wheel over and repeat the process to make it true.*

176. *Making a backcan. Mr F. Shields, Redmire, Wensleydale, having marked round the pattern on a sheet of tin, cuts out the required shape with a pair of tinman's snips.*

177. *Breaking the tin by putting it twice through rollers to smooth it.*

178. *Seaming front to back. Called a locked joint, the edges are turned over in opposite directions and then interlocked.*

179. *Jennying the back of the top. This makes a lip, ready for seaming.*

180. *Turning loops and handles for wiring.*

181. *Cutting bosses for side handles. The boss fits inside the handle to make an easy grip. Note the three stakes.*

182. *Turning top front seam with pliers to close the gap. The tinsmith stands on a box and the backcan is on an extension stake.*

183. *Soldering on handles.*

TINSMITH MAKING A BACKCAN

191. *Leading stone from Shipley Quarry, Cotherstone, Teesdale (1920s).*

QUARRYING &

193. *Mr T. Joy points out smout-holes at the foot of a wall built by him on Grassington Moor, Wharfedale.*

SMOUT-HOLES

92. *Typical Dales' roofs of stone slates.*
Mr T. T. Dinsdale and his son, Gayle,
Wensleydale, re-roofing a house at
Askrigg.

ROOFING

94. *Stile near Hawes, Wensleydale.*

STILE

STILES

195. *Barrel-shaped stile at Askrigg, Wensleydale.*

196. *Stile with six treads near Horton-in-Ribblesdale.*

The all round work of the craftsmen is shown by a close look at the work carried out over the years by the Winsbys of Leyburn. From a number of ledgers, the earliest dating from 1775, it may be inferred that they started as joiners and wheelwrights, changing to cabinet makers with Thomas Winsby (1811–1890).

John Winsby (1778–1851) specializing in work on the farm was the agricultural engineer of his time in Leyburn. His major undertakings were the repair of four-wheeled wagons with spring poles and the making of carts, coups, sweeps, harrows and ploughs. Besides small objects such as pig troughs, he made the then existing 'threshers' and winnowing machines, and supplied iron ploughs in a district where the pastoral country of the dales abutted on to the arable land of the Vale. He fitted the wagons, chiefly belonging to millers, with new broad wheels at £4 10s. the pair, or with new bodies painted red and 'Prushanblue' costing £5 5s. On some days he was 'riving spokes' and frequent work included 'wheels axling' and 'wheeles rung round'. In between he made 'ratten' traps, doors, gates, windows, coffins, a necessary (privy) seat 10 ft. 6 ins. long, a rug frame, parts of a loom owned by a Leyburn grocer and draper and a guide post which, painted with forty-four letters, cost £1. As with all the other Winsbys up to 1948, he had land and kept stock. After 1830 he became innkeeper at the Crown Inn, Leyburn.

His son, Thomas Winsby (1811–1890) cabinet maker, was an outstanding craftsman, who none the less undertook all kinds of work. From one of his ledgers covering the first few years of the reign of Victoria we read that a 'Coutch' cost 17s.; '8 Mirican Birtch chairs with hair Bottoms' sold at 14s. apiece; a 'new Bed-stead with Inge pools [poles] and Teastor' could be had for £1 8s. 5½d.; a 'Rosewod Wat Not' cost £3 5s. Sometimes people were refurnishing and he supplied a 'New Oke press with Coullams do. pannels cross-banded with mahogany' for £7 7s., a 'New Mahogany Chist of drwrs with Collums and fries' for £5 8s. and a new mahogany wardrobe for £9 9s. Sometimes Thomas bought a tree from a landowner and, as shown in the following entry, eventually when seasoned it was used for a specific job. '1840 Dec. 9 To Selfe and Robrt. one day saging [sawing] Larch for Sawfa. Dec. 21 To New sofa makeing with larch 17s. 9¾d. Time makeing Sofa and Cuching £1 4s.'

During the period covered by the one ledger Thomas and his men worked for an average of 4d. an hour, 3s. 6d. a day for a man and 1s. for a lad. Bills were sent out once a year. Occasionally debts were settled in kind, milk, potatoes, or coal or quarts of blackberries, but this was not general practice.

In the latter half of the nineteenth century three families of Winsbys, employing many men, worked as joiners and cabinet makers in Leyburn. At the workshop which still remains, there were within recollection eight cabinet makers, an

upholsterer and a polisher; and the re-dressing by machinery of old hair and wool
mattresses was advertised. Furniture was displayed on the roadside in front of the
shop on market days. The present Mr John Winsby, craftsman and antique dealer,
has made many fine pieces, especially desks. He cherishes the first plane, which he
was given to practise with as a child, and keeps the rule of sharpening his tools at
night ready for use next morning.

In the Weatherald ledgers, dating from 1886–1918, entries of funerals and
coffins give prices and customs. In 1894 an infant's coffin cost 1s. 6d., and in 1887
a polished pitch pine coffin with breast plate and handles, lined with cotton wool
and shroud, cost £2 18s. 6d., but a polished oak coffin with special lining and
shroud cost £6 8s. Not only did the funeral expenses include the coffin and
conducting the funeral but also distributing funeral cards and bidding, sometimes
providing biscuits, or the ingredients for making them, occasionally pairs of
gloves (ten pairs were ordered in 1894 at 2s. 11d. a pair). Arranging for the
'knowling' (tolling) bell cost 1s.

Formerly the wheelwright kept stored in his workshop the component parts of
a wheel—ash for the felloes, roughly shaped pieces of oak for the spokes and
blocks of elm for the *nafs* (hubs) seasoned for at least seven years, although even in
1806 Richard Garth, of Swaledale, records in his diary that he went to Tan hill in
July for '2 *gang* [sets] of spokes and naves from Robt. Langstaff, Brough'. Latterly
all the different parts were bought.

In October 1967 Mr W. T. Thompson, joiner at Hawes, Wensleydale, made a
cart wheel for us. He had not made one since 1935, yet the work went through
without the slightest hesitation (*see plates* 154–61). As the work proceeded we
learnt that there were riven and sawn spokes, of which the former were the better,
that spokes, made of hickory, were bought ready-shaped for milk floats, as
were spokes for traps made of lancewood. Preparing spokes and felloes was a lad's
job in winter, and dowels, which pinned the felloes together, were sawn out of old
spokes with the paint cleaned off them. Nothing was wasted. A cart wheel took
four days to make and in 1935 cost £3 10s. for a pair.

In various districts the wheelwright shaped his spokes differently, and he could
recognize the sound of his own wheels as they rolled over the road. The secret of a
good wheel was to make it run on a plumb spoke, and when well made it lasted
thirty years without repair or re-tiring.

Some joiners specialized in the making of hayrakes. For instance in the 1930's
Mr Ernest Burton and his father at West Mill, Askrigg, Wensleydale, turning out
5,000 to 12,000 rakes a year, supplied them as far afield as Beverley and Newcastle.
At first the machines, bought from Prospect Mill, Hawes, now defunct, were
run by water power, but when an electricity plant was installed in 1908, they were

ingeniously converted to be run by electricity. On one machine Ernest Burton remembers making 1,000 rake shafts in a day. West Mill is now disused.

At Dent Town Mr R. Haygarth, joiner and undertaker, still makes about forty-five dozen a year. Up to 1930 when it was usual to see joiners standing selling hay-rakes at local markets, two other men in Dent earned a living making them working full time all the year round. Just as the large scythes have gone, so rakes with sixteen to eighteen teeth have been superseded by the twelve-tooth head. In 1900 a hayrake with a pitch-pine shaft sold for 1od. Now one with a Douglas fir handle (pitch-pine would be prohibitive) costs 8s. 6d.[1]

Bought from local farmers, about a dozen straight strong ash trees, growing in open woodland, are felled each year. The best grained wood is reserved for rake bows, and the rest kept for the heads. English elm, from trees whose boles should not be more than 9 ins. to 10 ins. in diameter, is suitable for the teeth. Shafts, formerly cut in the workshop and rounded with the rounding plane, were turned out eight per hour. At first worked by a large paraffin engine and then by electricity, machinery is now used. To make the bows lengths of wood are steam heated for thirty minutes, bent with a bow bending jig and then bent over the *former*, a smooth even log about 10 ins. in diameter, and lastly stored on racks (*see plates* 162–6).

Finally the three main parts of a rake—the shaft, head and bow—are quickly fitted together, the finished rakes bound up in bundles of six, and dispatched for sale.

[1] *Hay rake making in Dent*. R. Haygarth. (Thesis.)

BLACKSMITHS & TINSMITHS

FORMERLY almost every village had a blacksmith to whom at one time or another all the inhabitants turned for shoeing their horses, for repair work and for making all manner of iron-work. In the dales the number of smiths was swollen by those employed at the lead-mines: there were five in 1823 at Gunnerside, Swaledale, and six at both Redmire and Preston-under-Scar, Wensleydale, all mining villages. Many also combined the occupation with that of innkeeper: out of nine families of blacksmiths at Askrigg, Wensleydale, during the last century four followed the two trades. But apart from this and work for industry a village blacksmith, although he might specialize, was occupied with two distinct branches of his craft—the farrier's work of shoeing horses and the general smith's work, which included the hooping of cart wheels. This and shoeing in general formed the mainstay of his livelihood.

When men like Mr Joe Holmes of Austwick, Craven, served their apprenticeship, earning 2s. a week, work with horses was paramount. 'Ah've been at t' back o' t' anvil for fifty-six years,' he says. On shoeing horses Mr J. J. Tallon, Middleton, near Sedbergh, explained that 'You mustn't be windy of a horse. They know. I've never been bet. If a rearing and kicking horse is bad to shoe, put a rope round its neck and others at each side round the back legs, so that when two men pull, the fetlocks are drawn in and the horse goes down.'

Similarly Mr J. Robinson, former blacksmith of Redmire, Wensleydale, remembers the awkward task of shoeing cows, which were often shod on the farm before being driven a distance. The beast was tied up and a six-foot pole put between its hind legs, which were the most difficult to do. When this was given a twist the leg came up, and the cloven hoof was shod with two small separate plates.

Mr R. B. Spencer, blacksmith of Hawes, Wensleydale, where there is now one forge, has vividly pictured the heyday of the farrier and his near demise in the 1950's: 'When I was apprenticed in 1922, there were two forges in t' smithy, two next door and one in the Holme. The first job on a morning was to light the fire. On Tuesday, market day, horses and traps and horses and carts were coming in from all the dales. They wanted 'em shoeing time they were in. There were stables behind every inn and ostlers at the Crown and the White Hart. Farmers paid 6d. to have their horses looked after. We used to have a list and take 'em i' turn. We'd go to the stables, where t' hosses were tied i' rows, facing forward so that nobody was kicked; we knew 'em all bi sight or bi name. I could shoe ten horses, all four feet, in a day from eight in a morning until eight at night—it was a killer. And they were not allus quiet. The worst of the last horse was that it was allus a bad 'un.

'At hay-time they wouldn't bring 'em in to shoe until they wanted 'em, so they all came together. I've seen 'em many a time queuing right up to the Penny Garth. We were on shoeing horses every day for three weeks. In 1948 there was only one tractor in the locality. By 1958 they'd all got 'em.'

Even if the traditional work of the farrier and with it the making of ironwork for carts and the hooping of wheels has gone, many blacksmith's shops, however modern their equipment, still have horseshoes and old tools, such as swages to make pokers, hanging from the beams and the flotsam of centuries collected round the hearth and *stiddy* (anvil). From underneath a work-bench under a window a seat swivelled out and, sitting on it, the smith sharpened the points of horseshoe nails on a small anvil fixed in a hole in the bench.

Many smithies have a hearth five feet square, large enough to heat a hoop for tiring a wheel, with a fire at each end and two pairs of bellows, left- and right-hand. Outside near the front door may be found two square-sided iron staples fixed in a huge heavy stone sunk level with the ground. Under these the tire hoops, long narrow lengths of iron, were levered and bent into rounds. There are iron stands or large flat stones to take a wheel with the hole in the centre for tiring. Alongside that at Gunnerside smithy, Swaledale, is a slake trough into which a stream has been diverted to keep it filled with water to cool and contract the iron hoop round the wheel.

Mr J. J. and Mr J. H. Tallon, of Sedbergh and Middleton, who occasionally re-tire wheels for the caravans of gipsies passing through on their way to the West-morland fairs, hooped one for us in 1966 (*see plates* 169–75). The smith, working with the wheelwright, often hooped six or eight wheels in a day. 'I've seen 'em red raw wi' it'; and children roasted chestnuts in the hot fire.

From the day books of David Calvert of Gunnerside, dating from 1871 to 1896, a picture may be formed of the work of the smith, much of it seasonal and much of it personal to individual customers. Especially on the frosty days of January many horses were brought to have their shoes *sharped* and *spurned*, that is, each shoe was removed, sharpened all over including the heel, and a spurn, a bar across the toe, fixed to prevent slipping. The sharping of four shoes cost 1s. In late spring tar marks at 8d. were ordered and horn burns at 1s. 6d. which were tried out on the wooden doors of the shop. In May loads of coal bought by the corve were fetched from William Gill Pit. In June the smith supplied sheep shears at 2s. or he ground old ones on the grindstone, always a feature of a smithy, for 1d. or 2d. In early July many men came to buy new scythes at 5s. or 6s. 8d. each, new shafts at 1s., grass nails for 2d. and hayforks from ones seven feet long at 3s. 9d. to small ones at 2s. 2d., whilst repairing 'moing machines' was frequent.

Besides these a random selection of entries shows the delightful phonetic spelling, the Swaledale nicknames and the miscellaneous nature of the jobs:

James Alderson Lump Nee Horse 2 shoes 2 sprd [spurned]	4d
Thom Buxton Nancy Tom New Gallow Shoeing	1s 2d
Charley Will Bobs 1 old Shoe	4d
Jack Rutter's Cudey Come [curry comb] Mending	2d
Maty Jone Ned Sled Chane Mending	2d
Jamey Trouper Jd Wiffe Ketel Lid Nop [knob] put on	2d
Joseph Coty Bety Key Mending for Chiney Case	4d
James Persivels 2 old Horn Burns to Mark Chees JW & HC	2s 0d
Muker Docktor Brass tap mending	6d
Jefery Heseltine Mrs Sepecttiles mending	4d
Jim Parker 2 Heters for etilian iron of your iron	6d
Edward Broadrake New Swape for Coffey Mill	6d
Edward Broadrake Brass Screw Making for Line Drawing Insterment	6d
Tazey Jack Will Dother Clogs repairing 2 plates etc.	2d
Joseph Alderson Baxton Beul Lizing Reviting on	6d
[The handle of an iron bakstone laying and riveting on]	
Thom Rutter for thistlebout [a farm] New Range Making with Let down Bar	
45 lb.	18s 9d
Paul Tenon Chesferd put up together 2 new Girths	1s 0d
[Cheese vat re-made and re-hooped]	
Kit Miller Dother man Wood Leg Plates for gig	10d

Like all craftsmen David Calvert ran a small farm as his descendants at Gunnerside do to this day, and farming or personal items punctuate the entries in the day book for 1871. In February he wrote: 'Me poorly soarthroat of[f] work'; in March he was 'On Getening out Muck'; in May, again poorly, he wrote, 'Me was [worse] than nothing'. In July they started 'Moing for hay'; in August 'Jas [James, one of his sons] of[f] for Load Ling after noon'; in September David and James [his sons] were 'At Westend Nitton [nutting, gathering hazel-nuts]': in October he was 'On whitening smithy' a few days before Gunnerside Fair; and on 25th December he wrote 'Cri Mas day Holaday'.

The blacksmith, now greatly diminished in numbers, has turned to other work such as plumbing, and is aided by an electric blower for the forge and by electric drills, grinders and oxy-acetylene welders. Yet he still shoes a few riding ponies and racehorses where there are racing stables and he exerts his skills in dealing with red-hot metal from sharpening and tempering tools to making hand-forged decorative iron-work.

Compared with blacksmiths, tinsmiths chiefly based on the market towns were rare. Mr F. Shields and his sons, descendants of a tinner and brazier at Middleham in the 1820's, live at Redmire, Wensleydale, and are now largely occupied as plumbers and oil-fired heating engineers. Yet, although not often used as such, the tinsmith's workshop remains near Bolton Castle. Before this was in use Frank Shields' grandfather lived and worked in the castle itself, and plumber and glazier as well as tinsmith, he cast sheet lead in the vaults. Prior to the First World War the Shields carried goods by horse and flat cart to huts which they had at Carperby, West Burton and Thoralby. They visited Askrigg once a week and sent their wares into Dent and Swaledale.

Over the years the workshop has changed very little. On the walls hang metal patterns for making dishes, pans, pails, loaf tins, coal hods and cans of all descriptions, including teacans, complete with spout and lid, used at hay-time. There is a pattern for a heather-burner which, containing paraffin, was and is used by game-keepers to fire the ling. Here, too were made the copper kettles traditionally given as prizes for the sports at local feasts—only the spouts and handles were bought.

Each pattern has written on it necessary measurements and directions for cutting out and also a note of the name and address of the person for whom it was first produced. On high shelves and on the floor are stored the metal pans which fit at the back of the special plumber's stove, stags' horns from which handles may be fashioned and casting tongs for lifting hot lead. On the main work-bench under the window there are different sized holes to take the attachments to which extendable 'heads'—metal objects over which tinned plate is hammered—are fitted, and in which stakes, the tinsmith's anvils, may be fixed. The 'heads' and stakes, kept on shelves under the benches, are brought up on the crook of the arm. As in any craftsman's workshop everything has its place. If you waste five minutes looking for something 'it shows in the end'.

Against another wall is the roller which resembles a small mangle, through which a piece of tin put through twice is 'broken' to ensure a smooth finish. Alongside are the folders, in which the tin, previously cut into shape, is folded ready for seaming the edges together. The jenny, which has several uses, mainly turning edges on the sides and bottoms of round articles, fastening wire into the tin for strengthening purposes, and making patterns on the finished parts, is sited in good light under the window (*see plates* 176–83).

As in all skilled work there are certain practices which become second nature to the experienced tinsmith. For instance, all corners of tin, however small, even discarded pieces, must always be snipped off with shears in order to prevent danger from sharp edges. When choosing the size of a sheet of tin, it must be related to the article or series of articles being made so as to prevent wastage. Every moment adds to costs, so that work is carried out in an economical and correct order. When hammering tin, it must always be done over a 'head', that is against something solid, or it will be spoilt, and when seaming edges together, if the top of the article is held away from you, it will automatically come right. Soldering is carried out as the work proceeds because if left to be finished all at once, the fire will die down and time will be lost; and it is simple to set something square by eye by putting it in line with something already square such as a window pane. These are a few of the practices which an apprentice has to learn.

In October 1965 Frank Shields made us a backcan to hold seven gallons of milk. Plates 176–83 show some of the procedure. It is possible to make one in six hours, but seven is usual, and the best progress is made during the first hour and a half. It used to be reckoned that if the top was on and turned but not soldered by dinner time, you were right. Every part has to fit exactly, and when it is made it is polished with Paris white—a lad's job. Even for this there is a right way and a wrong way. Polishing begins at the bottom and finishes at the top. In the 1920's a backcan sold for 16s. 6d., and ours, a beautiful piece of craftsmanship, cost £4 10s.

STONE MASONS, WALLERS
& DRAINERS

EVEN in the stone country of the Yorkshire dales masons were never a numerous band of craftsmen, and recently so little work existed for them that for fifty, indeed almost a hundred, years they were only rarely to be found. Serving an apprenticeship and often following his father in the trade, the mason learnt his craft from an early age and might as a child be given a small chisel and hammer with which to practise.

Like the blacksmith the number of masons was swollen, particularly before and about the middle of the last century, by employment in the lead-mines where in the arches of ruined smelt mills his skills may still be seen. Largely outdoor work affected by bad weather conditions, his was an occupation fraught with economic hazard. Masons liked to have a headstone to carve in winter, even keeping one in the parlour.

Allied with the occupation of mason, and latterly often combined with it, was that of quarryman. The quarries, each with its known reputation for good or poor, hard or soft, stone usually sandstone, remain to be seen. To name a few, all now disused, there were Shipley quarry at Cotherstone, Teesdale, Hill Top at the head of Swaledale, Stagsfell near Hawes and Mileanhour near Carperby, Wensleydale, Scotgate Ash and Moorhouses near Pateley Bridge, and others at Burtersett, Wensleydale. Stone from the three latter, especially Scotgate flourishing in the last century and the beginning of this, was sent all over the country, for instance for the construction of the Albert Memorial and the National Gallery, London. But whether used nationally or locally the stone was dressed at the quarries at benches called bankers and by masons known as banker hands.

Roofing stone, lifted off by the bed, was got in certain quarries where fissile material was available. Some of the most noted, whence slates were sent all over the surrounding districts, were near West Scrafton, Coverdale. Here, Gilbert Scar and other quarries worked up to about seventy years ago, were approached by levels (galleries) and the slabs of stone to be split into smooth thin slates or flags were brought out by wagons running on rails.

Whilst early generations of masons were engaged on abbey, church and bridge building, a later generation built the schools and the Wesleyan chapels of the last century. It is remembered that the father and uncle of Mr T. T. Dinsdale of Gayle, Wensleydale, helped to build Marsett Chapel, Semerdale, walking the four miles there and back from Gayle over Wether Fell and earning 2s. 6d. and 2s. 3d. a day respectively. On the other hand we have a record of 1710 for the building of a stable, probably at Thornton Rust, when the building of walls was paid for at the rate of 8d. a day plus 'meat'.

Direct descendants of masons engaged on work in the lead-mines are the Peacocks of Castle Bolton, who coming from Swaledale to arch levels in the Wensleydale mines about 1830, stayed in that dale. As the family still does, they rented Bolton Greets in Apedale, a quarry yielding excellent freestone, for 2s. 6d. a year from Lord Bolton. Up to the Second World War they regularly spent a month there each year, and because of a seam of coal at hand they were able to improvise a forge and sharpen picks and other tools on the spot. A suitable area of stone, known as a post, is quarried by means of nicking with a freestone pick, then using wedges placed nine inches apart, knocked by a 14-lb. sledge hammer until the stone starts to lift. This process is repeated to cut the stone to size and large blocks were lifted by a gantry and a lewis—an iron contrivance with a ring at the top wedged into the stone. When roughly dressed, usually for quoins or sills, the stone was brought down by horse and cart with a sledge load of stones behind it to act as brake.

In building a house the first requirement is to have good quoins, set plumb by using a line. A saying runs, 'A line and a rule, would guide a fool'.[1] Again until the Second World War the walls of houses were built solid like field walls with two built-up sides, fillings, and with through-stones every yard. Cavity walls are a modern innovation as are damp courses in the dales. It was important to tilt the stones of house walls downwards by pinning them inside to throw the water out-wards. An eighteen inch thick wall is three inches higher inside than outside. Damp houses, of which there are many, the masons say were built badly by inexperienced hands.

Slating (and plastering) were formerly separate specialized crafts, and to obtain the correct pitch of a roof and to make each course diminish upwards evenly requires experience. 'If you don't set off right, you can't finish a roof', any mason will tell you. The slater begins at the eaves with large slates, the *undereasings* and *overeasings*, usually thirty-nine inches long and one and a half inches thick, placed on top of each other. These are *spelched* (tapered off at the bottom edge) and the upper flags, the overeasings, are an inch shorter than the lower. Graded upwards in size and thickness, the last slates next to the ridge stones are the *closers* or *spells*, perhaps

[1] Mr George Calvert, Pateley Bridge, Nidderdale.

three quarters of an inch thick and nine inches long. The slates overlap three and a half inches leaving the 'skirt' showing, and it is all too easy to have them 'head-bound', that is one riding on the top edge of the one below. Holes for nails to fasten them to the slate lats are made with hand picks specially tempered 'pigeon blue' by the blacksmith. To gauge where to put the slate lats, the slater lays a lat the length of the height of the roof on it, and with a slate ruler marks off the length of his slates, always remembering the overlap.

When he reaches a chimney, then the mason can show off. 'It should', says Mr Jim Peacock, 'be simple, about three feet high with a string course to keep the water off and with a blocking [the top] about four inches high and perhaps a pot.'

Stone floors were laid on a bed of sand. A peg was put in each corner of the room and, working to a long straight edge, the flags were placed across in rows, slightly higher than desired for the finish. Then they were tapped down level with a beater, something like a dolly stick. Occasionally bedroom and chamber floors were flagged.

Sometimes a mason constructed stiles, of which a number of fine examples are to be found in Wensleydale (*see plates* 194–5). Those near Gayle, difficult to date but perhaps put up at the time of the building of Hawes church near by in 1850, exhibit mason's marks. *Stoups* (monoliths) for gate-posts were quarried at Hill Top, Preston-under-Scar and elsewhere. About seven feet long tapering to the top, they were let into the ground about two feet six inches. Then the gate crooks or snecks were run in with lead. A hole was chiselled in the stone, the crook placed where required and a little cup of clay built round it. Then, using a special ladle with a very long handle, molten lead was poured in. It was necessary to stand side-ways as the lead might spit when it touched cold metal. It soon set; the clay was broken off and any surplus lead pared off.

Alas, stoup gate-posts and stoup stiles are unlikely ever to be made again, just as it would be hard to conceive of the drystone walls being built under present day conditions. The men who built these were wallers not masons by trade and the period of the enclosures of the commons, the early years of the last century, was their heyday.

Recollections of the building of long lengths of wall, let out in contracts, have been handed down especially in Dent. Often setting out in the dark the men walked miles to distant fells, earned 2s. 6d. or 3s. a rood of seven yards, regarded as a day's work, and in order to *addle* a living ate their oatcake and raw bacon as they worked. Two brothers by the name of Petty, living at Arncliffe, Litton-dale, walled all summer building the new walls on the tops. Leaving home at 7 a.m. and taking a loaf and some onions as food, they built two roods a day and returned about seven o'clock at night. In the winter they earned a living doing odd jobs.

Walling is not difficult for a capable man with good hands and a straight eye. But there is a difference between the farmer who is able to wall a gap and the one who thinks of his work as a craft, who likes a wall to look well because it will be there for years.

Such men, describing the method, say that the footings must be good, or 'you're never right', that the courses must be even, and that you wall 'one over two and two over three', that is, cross the joints. Ideally two men work at each side, for a fence consists of double walls with the space between packed with flakes of stone—the fillings. If a man works alone, he changes sides, or if for some reason, such as rising ground, he cannot, he walls 'overhand' from one side. A wall should start at the bottom about two feet six inches wide and batter to about a foot with three rows of throughs in it. At the end of his work he runs his eye along the topstones (*capes* in the North Riding) to see if they are dead level.

Mr Thomas Joy of Grassington, Wharfedale, a waller of the old school, says that he inherited his craft from his mother's side of the family. 'I never use a line and the hammer as little as possible. Fillings by rights should be put in individually, not thrown in, and you must leave a space the thickness of a finger at the top of them, so that the topstones lie flat and don't rock. I like topstones to project a bit at each side; the same with throughs. They strengthen a wall and stop sheep from jumping over.' On one wall he has placed a through so that a little hollow in it collects water for the birds.

A waller has an eye for walling stones and sees a good through even if only its nose is sticking out of the ground. 'He's a good binder.' Thomas Joy has carried many a heavy through long distances on his back. Millstone grit outcrops were sources of them in many parts of the dales; and in limestone country thousands were fetched from areas such as Cow Close, Littondale.

Every wall is a gauge of the geology of a district, being composed of sandstone, limestone or slate as the underlying stratum dictates, and many are examples of craftsmanship. Every dalesman knows where there are good walls which have stood sixty to a hundred years and never budged.

Draining the land was practised extensively in the last century either by a man himself improving his farm even if he were a tenant or by professional drainers working for the landlord in gangs of twenty or thirty men. Fifty years ago there were Taylors, Ivesons and Kirkbrides, drainers at Gayle, Wensleydale, who might walk eight or ten miles to work in winter and earn 9d. a rood.[1] In summer they

[1] Mr W. G. Wallbank, Keasden, remembers 1s. or 1s. 6d. being paid.

turned to walling. A Ribblesdale man and his brother once surprised their employer by cutting thirteen roods before breakfast. Drainers wore clogs with steel plates on the instep, a steel band round the sides and a steel plate on the toe-cap. Tom Twistleton writes in 'T' Kersmas Party':

> *Some dance wi' eease i' splendid style,*
> *Wi' tightly-fitting togs on;*
> *Whal others bump about au t'while,*
> *Like drainers wi' their clogs on.*

Of the several types of drain—open, stone, shoulder, tile, and sod or bog—the last is still carried out precisely as it was described by Tuke in *General View of Agriculture of the North Riding* (1794) (*see plates 199–202, taken in 1965*). In sod draining, which is suited to clay soils, the drainer employs a long drainer, Tom spade and two scoops with six-foot-long handles—a topping scoop 1 ft. 4 ins. long and a bottoming scoop 1 foot long. The latter is for nicking and cleaning out the bottom. Made by the blacksmith, these were fitted to suit a man like a scythe—with the drainer holding the handle on the hip the scoop itself should lie flat on the ground.

For the shoulder drain a ledge is made part way down the trench and stones laid across it leaving a channel below them. The stone drain has no shoulder. It may be any depth, depending on the ground to be drained. Whatever stones are to hand, perhaps from a beck, are laid in the bottom, built up at the sides and others placed on top, making a channel about six inches square. The trench is then filled up. If the bottom is hard only side and top stones are necessary. Serving three purposes they drain the water from the top, from the sides and form a conduit to carry it away. Tile draining, often deemed less efficacious than stone, was none the less commonly practised and in the last century thousands of tiles were made at local tileries, such as those at Gargrave and at Redmire, Wensleydale.

Open or moor draining, usually called *gripping*, meant digging an open trench about 2 ft. 6 ins. wide and 1 ft. deep tapering to a point at the bottom. The drainer started by taking a string a chain (22 yds.) long, and with a gripping spade, razor-sharp on the long side, he cut, using a sawing action through heather, roots and peat without lifting out the spade. Having finished one side, he started back again down the other, and finally pulled out the turfs with a muck fork. 'I've cut many a mile,' says Mr W. E. Iceton of Baldersdale.

197. *Mr John Hunter walling a gap on the Buttertubs Pass.*

198. *Mr John Mattinson, West Riding County Council roadman, using a walling-frame while building a new wall of Silurian slate at Studfold, Ribblesdale. Road widening is causing the building of long lengths of new walls.*

199. *Mr Gordon and Mr George Wallbank, sod draining on High Birks Farm, near Clapham. They have nicked down each side with a Tom spade and are removing the turf.*

200. *The sod in the centre has been nicked slantwise by the Tom spade by standing on the left and nicking on the opposite side of the sod and vice versa. The sods are being dug out and placed on one side.*

SOD DRAINING

201. *Digging the trench down to water, $2\frac{1}{2}$ ft to 3 ft deep, with a draining spade.*

202. *Having scooped out the bottom of the trench with the scoop the drainer treads down the sods placed upside-down and the trench is filled in.*

203. *Mr T. W. Thacker, Bedale, wearing a thread apron, twisting hemp thread.*

204. *Mr Thacker sewing with leather held in a clamp.*

SADDLERS

205. *Mr H. J. Howard, Gargrave, using a half-moon knife.*

206. *Mr R. L. Peart, Gilling, near Richmond, repairing a saddle.*

207. *Mr Tommy Hunter, Redmire, Wensleydale, demonstrates his sewing machine, formerly used for stitching the uppers.*

208. *Mr Hunter sharpening a knife in his workshop.*

209. *Mr Christopher Binks, Carlton-in-Coverdale, and lasts.*

BOOT &

210. *Mr Arthur Inman, Grassington, Wharfedale, moulding the sole to the insole with a hammer and using a stirrup.*

211. *Mr F. Ward, Leyburn, sewing on the welt (1957).*

212. *Mr Hunter putting nails into a boot-sole; on the left, a rack and lasts (there used to be fifty to sixty pairs) and below, a seat for customers or friends.*

SHOEMAKERS

C L O G G E R S   *213. Mr M. D. Grainger of Hawes shaping clog soles (c. 1950).*

214. Mr J. V. Brown of Airton, Malhamdale, demonstrates the use of the clogger's stiddy.

215. Mr Myles Bainbridge of Sedbergh fits the upper to the sole.

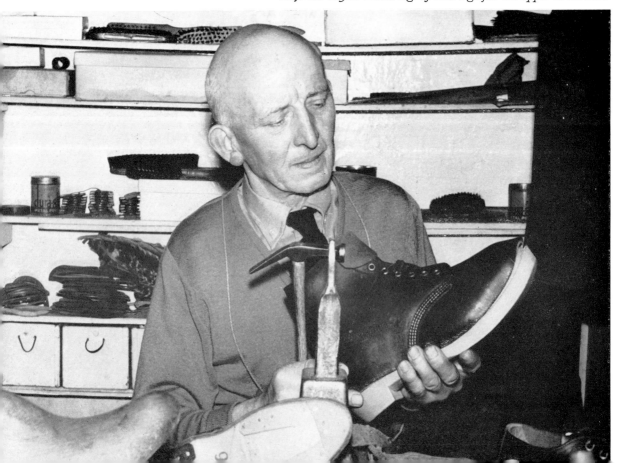

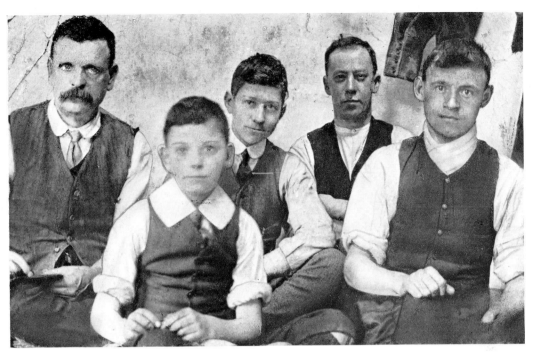

216. *Tailors sitting on the board at Martland's tailor's shop, Hawes, in 1913. From left to right: A journeyman tailor, two apprentices, Mr R. R. T. Hind and Mr J. F. Thompson, Mr H. F. Martland (Master Tailor) and Mr R. Staveley.*

217. *Mr C. J. Murphy and his son Mr C. Murphy of Richmond, sitting cross-legged on the board.*

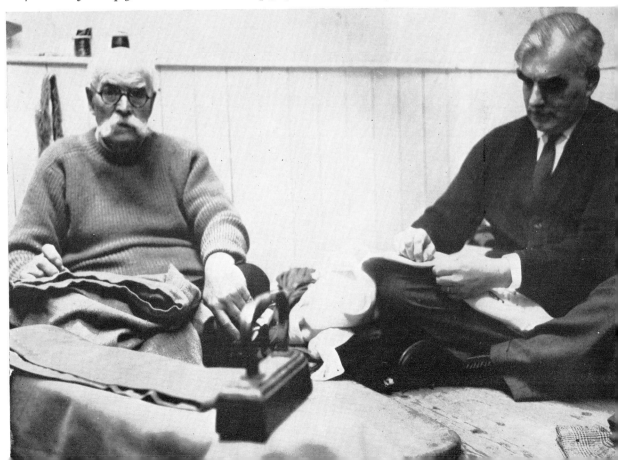

218. *Mr W. R. Outhwaite (1875–1956), Hawes, Wensleydale, at the big wheel, spinning the warps with which to make yarn for weaving into webbing (c. 1941). The warps stretch the length of the rope-walk.*

219. *Mr W. R. Outhwaite and his son, Mr T. G. Outhwaite, scaling—preparing yarn for weaving into webbing (c. 1941).*

MAKING WEBBING

220. *Weaving webbing for halters, backbands, hopples, etc., in the rope-maker's workshop (c. 1941).*

221. *Mr T. G. Outhwaite, Hawes, making ropes.*
He is winding the handle of the sledge which puts the
back twist in, i.e. tightens up the twist already made.

222. *Making cow bands for tying up cows. The*
rope-maker uses a small cow's horn to separate the
strands to make a loop at one end.

ROPE MAKING

223. *The rope-maker's workshop. Mr Outhwaite is making wagon ropes.*

224. *Mr J. Graham, Wath, Nidderdale, makes a band of ling, with which to tie up a loggin (batten).*

225. *Beginning to tie up the loggin.*

226. *Pulling the band tight.*

227. *A loggin tied up.*

PREPARATION FOR LING THATCHING

228. *Thatched house, Colsterdale (1938), since burnt down. The sods are shown on the ridge and the hazel rods down the sides.*

229. *Levy Pool, near Bowes. Mr T. Robinson and his family, photographed about 1916. The house has a door-head dated GHA 1736, and was last occupied by Mr and Mrs J. Addison in 1925.*

LING-THATCHED HOUSES

230. *Ling-thatched Hoghouse, Summer Lodge, Swaledale (1941).*

LING-THATCHED BARNS

231. *Barden Scale Barn, Wharfedale, cruck-built and ling-thatched, partially dismantled for removal to Shibden Hall Museum, Halifax, where it was accidentally destroyed by fire.*

232. *East Stoney Keld, near Bowes, showing construction of roof timbers for ling thatch.*

BESOM MAKING

233. *Mr John Lister (1870–1961) raising ash spells (bands) by hammering.*

234. *John Lister using the besom engine and needle to bind besoms with the spells.*

235. *Mr J. W. Ra*
of Dent, hedging
in Garsdale.

236. *Mr R. H. Joh*
of Gawthrop, Dent.

237. *Mr G. Ellis,*
Hacra Farm,
hedging in Dent.

238. *Mr R. Ridding*
of Gawthrop, Dent,
hedger, waller
and paver.

239. *Stick making. Mr F. Graham, Grimes Gill, Masham Moor, with shafts and completed sticks.*

240. *Preparing the horn for fixing on the shaft.*

STICK MAKERS

241. *Mr W. Sutcliffe, Horton-in-Ribblesdale.*

242. *Mr E. Harper, Sedbergh.*

SADDLERS, SHOEMAKERS
& CLOGGERS

NEVER a numerous class of craftsmen, not one saddler is now left in the dales proper. The nearest, Mr T. W. Thacker, is at Bedale. We have talked to four others, now retired or semi-retired: Mr R. L. Peart whose father was apprenticed to the firm of King at Richmond; Mr L. Curtis who worked for Myers, Richmond; Mr B. Procter who was apprenticed to William Gilchrist at Settle; and Mr H. J. Howard of Gargrave, who came from Norfolk where his family had been saddlers for generations. When Bert Procter began his apprenticeship in 1903, there were six saddlers in Settle; when he retired in 1958 he was the only one for many miles round and had no more than a day's work in a week.

Saddlery was divided into harness, saddle and collar making. Or a saddler might be classified as brown or black—the first making saddles and bridles for hunters and racehorses and the second harness for heavy cart or dray horses. But as work diminished the country saddler, even though he might well excel in one particular branch, undertook all kinds of work. For instance the saddler at Hawes, Wensleydale, made embossed leather fishing creels and one at Sedbergh made hedging gloves. Those who lived on the edges of the dales visited arable farms to repair the harness of the twelve to fifteen horses kept on them. On this work Mr R. L. Peart earned 10s. a day, his keep and the cost of the materials. Journeymen saddlers, carrying their tools and travelling round seeking work were said to be 'cracking the whip'.

Bert Procter recalls that as an apprentice he was paid 2s. 6d. a week and afterwards $4\frac{1}{2}$d. an hour for a day beginning at 7 a.m. and ending at 6 p.m. Discipline was severe. Once when he dropped a pair of hames he was asked: 'If you were at home would you drop a piece of furniture?'

An apprentice's first job was to make wax ends. 'I've waxed many a thousand ends and done it all day Sunday,' R. L. Peart recalls. Saddlers formerly used beeswax but also made their own wax from 1 lb. pitch, $\frac{1}{2}$ lb. resin and a little tallow. The ends of the sewing thread, made from several lengths of hemp according to the requirements of the work in hand and twisted together, were waxed. Next the apprentices were often put on to repair work and then to learning to sew straight and evenly along the ridge strap which fits along the horse's back to the crupper. Besides the actual work, they learnt which parts of a hide were used for the different pieces of harness.

Sewing varied from five to fourteen stitches to an inch. Bert Procter tells us that although fine work took longer, he averaged six feet of sewing an hour at six stitches to the inch, and has easily finished 40 ft. of sewing in a day, at times working by the light of three oil lamps or candles. To cut out and sew a full length pair of traces, about six feet long, which have four rows of stitching, nine stitches to the inch, sewn through three or four thicknesses of leather, took the best part of two days to finish. All saddlers have worn a callous on the palm of their right hands with the awl, and grooves down to the bone of their little fingers with pulling the threads tight. (They sew with two needles passing the threads in different directions through the same hole.)

The harness maker usually had a length book giving measurements for every type of harness from that for a four-in-hand to that for a donkey. But from experience he carried most measurements in his head. Usually keeping a large stock of goods, such as 1,000 buckles, he bought his 'furniture' from firms at Walsall who regularly issued *Equine Albums*, comprehensive catalogues advertising anything from bits to horses' straw hats. Nowadays even the saddlery is bought from these firms in three sizes—pony, cob and full size—and altered to fit. Saddlers bought saddle trees from Hargrave's of Ripon, and noted for their ability to fit any horse, were regarded as the finest craftsmen using the best leather and the smallest stitches. Also skilled work, collar-making was the hardest. Each firm had a name ornament, a small brass plate engraved with their name and the town, and firms developed their own styles so that work differed slightly from one county to another.

In contrast to the rarity of saddlers, shoemakers, or cordwainers, as they were formerly called, were a numerous body of men. Villages had one to three and market towns six to eleven,[1] and the craft has not died out in the dales. Mr A. Inman, Grassington, Wharfedale and Mr F. Ward, Leyburn, Wensleydale, still make hand-made shoes.

Whilst the saddler worked on a high stool bracing his feet against a bar and holding a long clamp between his knees, the shoemaker using a shorter clamp sat on a low bench which incorporated space for his tools alongside. For braying leather for soles to make it close-grained, the cobbler used a lapstone, a smooth large flat pebble picked up from a beck.

A paragraph in the *Settle Chronicle* dated 1st September 1854 pictures an era when shoemakers bought their leather from local tanners who in turn bought their

[1] Directories of North and West Ridings of Yorkshire 1822, 1823, 1840.

hides from local butchers. Writing of the Settle Lammas Fair, the editor states that 'Some twenty years ago the 19th August was a day of great importance to the Curriers, Dealers and Shoemakers of this District. The neighbourhood of the Talbot Inn was crowded with the sons of Crispin and the sellers of Leather, and numerous traders in "Sparables" from that once great Shoe-nail mart, Silsden. It was no uncommon thing to see empty Leather waggons standing in the streets and Inn yards, whilst the bulky bundles of "Bend" were offered for sale in the Barns and Sheds of the Inn yard. Dealers and Shoemakers came from fifty to sixty miles round. This year the only relic of this once great Leather Fair were a couple of Silsden nailers.' Three reasons were given as the cause of the fair's decline: the establishment of a leather fair at Leeds, easier means of transit and the break-up of the twelve months' credit system in the shoe and leather trade.

Although in many families the craft of shoemaking was passed down by apprenticeship from father to son, many a farmer's son took it up for a living and hawked his wares for miles around. In this way the Wards started shoemaking two generations ago, and similarly Mr G. Robinson, Slaidburn, Bowland, learnt the craft from an Irishman who worked on the family farm, and who had been a gold medal bootmaker making boots for cowboys in America.

Mr W. Bayne remembers Joseph Allen of Lambparrocks, Dentdale, shoemaker and farmer, going to Lancaster with a horse and cart for leather leaving home at 3 a.m. and returning at 10 p.m. After making boots all the winter, employing two men, the Wards of Leyburn, Wensleydale, set off in a trap up Coverdale and over Dead Man's Hill into Nidderdale with a load of goods. Mr C. Binks, shoemaker of Carlton, Coverdale, also went into Nidderdale but at first on foot, and as each pair of boots weighed six or seven pounds, it was as much as he could carry to take three pairs at a time. His father used to start work at 4 a.m. and we were told thought the world of his measuring stick, beautifully made and folding flat, with which a customer's feet were measured. The Haws, a Wensleydale shoemaking family, based on Thoralby in the last century, employed four men and went 'reg'lar away' with a load of boots in a tub trap on rounds covering upper Wensleydale and Wharfedale. It was their boast that no boots were ever labelled, for every customer's order was remembered. When farmers bought a new pair, it was usual for them to order another, because they liked to hang them up for a year for the leather to season.

When we visited Mr Arthur Inman at Grassington in 1966, he was then eighty-two and engaged in making a fine hand-made pair of shoes. One of a large family, he was born at Thorpe, Wharfedale, where six great-uncles all of them shoemakers also lived. He served his apprenticeship at Skipton, and made his first pair of shoes for sale at the age of twelve. He recalls that when making farmers' boots, it was economical to work on several pairs at once. He spoke of journeymen seeking work at busy seasons, and said that it was worth paying them to sole a pair or two of boots, because they passed on new methods which they had picked up on their travels.

Both Arthur Inman and Frank Ward specialize in fine work and may charge £15 15s. for a pair of shoes which will take about twenty-eight hours to finish. On the other hand Christopher Binks and Tommy Hunter of Redmire, Wensleydale, no longer make boots, but continue with repair work, and neither of their workshops has changed since the day of the village shoemaker making women's, children's and men's strong and market boots.

Records of the Hunters as shoemakers go back to our knowledge to 1727 when a John Hunter of Norton, Co. Durham was apprenticed to a cordwainer. Besides the usual stipulations he was to be allowed 'Meat, Drink, Shows [Shoes], Apron, Washing and Lodging', and to receive 6d. at Easter, Whitsuntide and Christmas. More than a century later a Robert Hunter was a shoemaker at Askrigg, Wensleydale. In his account book, dating from 1840 to 1890, we learn that he had customers all over the dale and in Swaledale.[1] He made new boots, shoes and clogs, and repaired these and other leather goods. Part of his stock in trade included 'elastic' boots and 'sprin clogs' (lady's boots with wooden soles and heels with a leather 'waist' causing them to spring when walking). In 1851 it cost the vicar 1s. 6d. to have his 'shous heeld and spect' (patched) and the blacksmith 6d. to have his bellows mended. Bills were usually settled in part, sometimes paid off at 9d. or 1s. a month. Or items such as 'wife shoe stitched up heel 2d., trapping reins mended 5s., back-can strap stitched' were balanced against 'one pound of butter 1s. 1d., one back bone 1s. 3d., 2 lb. pork 1s.' and the difference paid in cash or allowed to run on to the next settlement.

The grandfather of Mr Thomas Hunter of Redmire and his brothers Jack and William were all shoemakers. But whether they are connected with the earlier Hunters we do not know. Tommy Hunter, starting when he was thirteen and now eighty-nine (1968) has worked in the same little cobbler's shop for seventy-six years. It contains a stove, lasts in an oak framework, a bench for customers, a long dresser and Delft rack holding tools, leather and paper patterns, a sewing machine, an old butter churn containing water, an oil lamp, a black pan for boiling up pitch, oil and resin to make wax and two, formerly three, cobblers' stools.

Once his father, uncle and himself were all at work in the shop and in order to make a living regularly went on until eight or nine o'clock at night by the light of the oil lamp or by candles stuck on the front of the benches. Morning and night two cows, kept on the pastures, had to be milked. Journeymen, usually soling

[1] MS. in the authors' possession.

four pairs of boots a week, earned 4s. a pair, paid 12s. for board and lodging and had 4s. left for beer and 'baccy'. In his father's early days hand-sewn boots sold for 12s. 6d. and within recollection at 18s. £3 was an agreed price after the First World War. When they bought the leather, they begged a sheepskin apron worth 2s. 6d. Ones made of calf skin were better, but they cost 10s.

Like shoemakers, cloggers served an apprenticeship. Mr Myles Bainbridge of Sedbergh, starting when he was fifteen, served his time at Yare's of Kirkby Stephen. In those days one of several men working for the firm was fully employed shaping clog-soles, which for many years now have been bought ready-made. Mr J. V. Brown of Airton, Malhamdale, who served his apprenticeship with his father and left because there was not enough work for two men, remembers that a beech tree of the right size was cut into suitable lengths, and each piece split in half lengthways made a pair of soles. Tommy Hunter speaks of eller (elder), good to cut, being used, whilst Mr G. Robinson of Slaidburn felled alder and silver birch grown on the farm. Alder was liked because being a soft wood it made a quiet clog. Sycamore, a light white wood, is used nowadays especially for women's clogs.

The soles were shaped with three clogging irons—a roughing out iron, a hollower and a gripper, all fixed as required on a stock (see plate 213). Left roughed out to dry for six to eight months, the soles were then hollowed out by the hollower and a channel along the outer edge on which the welts fitted was cut by the gripper. Formerly, too, the uppers were cut out in leather from patterns. Lastly they were calkered on the clogger's stiddy with calkers (irons) nailed on the sole. 'When making clogs', says George Robinson, 'you never put them down; to turn them toss them up in your hand.' With soles and uppers available, Myles Bainbridge could make twelve pairs in a day and always took particular pride in the shape. Latterly clog soles were bought from firms at Snaith, near Goole, and from Hebden Bridge in the West Riding, and clog irons, clasps, toe and heel plates, and clog uppers from James Horsfield of Bradford.

Clog markings used to be three sizes larger than for ordinary shoes and two sizes larger for children. There were clasp, bar and laced clogs—the clasps formerly of engraved brass. Laced were worn by men and boys and clasped by women and girls. Exhibition clogs might have french-polished soles and silver clasps and calkers.

Clogs are still worn, but not as they once were by everyone on the farm, by anyone engaged in wet indoor or outdoor work and by all school children well into the 1920's. Tommy Hunter told us: 'You really want bringing up wi' clogs. Youngsters used to wear 'em.' As Myles Bainbridge says, 'They are warm and airy, give plenty of room, don't pick up dirt like boots and don't slip on grass or on slimy flags.'

TAILORS

WHEN Singer put a reliable sewing machine on the market in 1851, wholesale clothing might be said to have begun. Yet it was possible to see a tailor sitting cross-legged sewing on a board at Hawes, Wensleydale, up to the 1960's.[1] Bespoke tailoring, like bespoke shoemaking, still continues. We have talked chiefly to the Murphys of Richmond and Mr A. Metcalfe and Mr F. Thompson of Hawes who remember the craft, its jargon and lore.

In the early years of the last century the population supported four, five and up to fifteen tailors in the market towns, and one or two in a few villages noted for their fairs. As late as 1890 there were six in Hawes.

In general tailors in the dales may be classified in four groups: the first, working in their own shops, who catered for the military and gentry, and the second for the better-end farmers and tradesmen. Then there were the journeymen, 'kicking for trade', who walked many miles all over the country working at tailors' shops and helping out in the busy seasons of the different regions. Lastly, the 'whip the cat' tailors who working on their own or with their wives, visited farms, and staying there repaired and made new suits from cloth provided by the farmer. Alexander Fothergill, diarist, of Carr End, near Semerwater, wrote on 29th December 1773: 'At home . . . had the Taylors March & Son makeing me a pair of Fustian gamashas [leggings] and Mending Cloaths etc.'

Like other craftsmen, tailors served their apprenticeship. Robert Staveley (1884–1965) of Gayle, Wensleydale, was apprenticed to Frank Weir, tailor of Hawes, and besides his keep was paid 6d. a week pocket money eventually raised to 1s. In 1909 at the age of fifteen Arnold Metcalfe was apprenticed to Weir's successor, E. Blythe, and has worked in the same premises ever since. The first objective was learning to sew straight; the first job was seaming linings for trousers; and the culmination of training was making a jacket. The sons of master tailors were trained as cutters, and for this purpose Mr C. J. Murphy (born 1883), who started his apprenticeship at the age of eleven, went to an academy in London. There were coat-hands (jacket-makers) who were the best craftsmen, and 'drummers' (trouser-

[1] Mr Robert Staveley up to his death in 1965 and Mr F. Thompson up to 1966.

makers) who were usually not good enough to make jackets. Vests (waistcoats), the easiest garments to make, were often given to the coat-hand to even out the work and pay.

Tailoring was formerly seasonal work. In Richmond where the busy season began in the spring and lasted throughout August, the tailors used to call 17th March Independence Day. On the other hand up the dales the season began at Whitsuntide, slacked off during hay-time and picked up again in the autumn.

Within recollection piece work was usual. At about the beginning of the century 9s. 6d. was paid for making a complete suit. Mr F. Thompson remembers earning 3s. for the vest, 3s. 6d. for the trousers and 6s. for the jacket. Mr A. Metcalfe says that just before the First World War a suit cost about 15s. 6d. in work, and plus cloth, trimmings and the boss's profit the total for one 'made on the board 'was from £2 to £3. Between the wars £1 was paid for making a jacket and 7s. 6d. for trousers, giving a wage of £2 to £2 10s. a week which, comparing favourably with the then current wages, was subject to seasonal falling off in custom.

In 1893 making uniforms for the Militia brought the Murphys to Richmond, where Michael Murphy was Master Tailor at the barracks with twenty men under him. Eight years later he set up at the present shop in Rosemary Lane. His son, Mr C. Murphy, recalls that a neighbouring tailor kept a 'grey hen' (large stoneware jar) filled with whisky in the middle of the floor for his largely sporting customers, and that many of the gentry not only did not pay their bills but borrowed money from their tailors. Other tailors with poorer clients remember that a funeral with its attendant mourning clothes often threw families into debt.

Regular numbers of men had permanent work in the shops and in busy seasons more were taken on. Sometimes the Murphys advertised in a Newcastle paper, and once a journeyman walked from Morpeth to Richmond and was found standing outside the shop in the early morning. Another wrote from Cornwall asking for work, and having bicycled all the way turned up two months later. Yet another came from Glasgow in the early summer and went on to Oban for the shooting and fishing season. The same men came round year by year.

Many had nicknames. One who had a red nose and took snuff and always came to Richmond during the hunting season was known as 'The Vinegar Plant'. Others were the 'Duke of Norfolk' and the 'One-eyed gunner'. Only too often they went 'on the cod' (a drinking spree), and living from hand to mouth were perpetually asking for 'something on the boot' (money on account). Occasionally one would arrive destitute and was helped by the tailors themselves having a whip round for him. Many ended their days in the 'grubber' (workhouse).

At Hawes, Wensleydale, the journeymen went to a lodging house of two rooms, one for the lodgers and one for the good-natured Mary Iveson who kept it and charged 3d. a night. As an apprentice Arnold Metcalfe was sent out to buy 3d. worth of liver which together with some onions the journeymen cooked in a pan supplied at the house.

All tailors, even the journeymen, provided their own tools: bodkin, thimble, small-point scissors for cutting button-holes and ripping out, pipeclay (chalk), beeswax for waxing linen thread and a straight-edge (measure). The thimble is without a top as the tailor pushes the needle with the front of it. They would not have been employed without tools, for borrowing would have wasted everybody's time.

We have seen a number of old tailors' workshops. The 'sitting boards', which vary in height from one to two feet from the ground, are sometimes placed round the walls with spaces in between or, resembling a stage, fill about three quarters of the room. Against a wall near the board is the special tailor's oven, a free standing stove, in which the tailor's 'goose' (iron) is heated. A horseshoe usually serves as a stand for the iron. Against another wall is a sewing machine or two and overhead hang a couple of lamps.

Work began at 7.00 or 7.30 a.m. and finished at the same times at night with two hours off for meals, except on Saturdays when work ended at three or four o'clock with half an hour's break. If a special order came in, hours were longer. Every morning when the tailors arrived they changed into 'sitting drums' (old patched trousers), then donned a pair of old slippers, took off their jackets and worked in their vests (waistcoats) and shirt sleeves. There might be seven or more of them on the board all sitting cross-legged. Old tailors went round pushing down the knees of apprentices. 'You sew on your knee; it's your anvil.' Many men could press a suit with a 30-lb. iron on a sleeve board on their knees and turning it over, press the other side. James Procter, tailor of Settle, at the age of eighty could put his feet round his neck. Nor were fingers less supple, although men with horny hands could sew well.

Some of the traditional slang has been remembered. An easy job or 'soft sew' was a 'nibble' or 'moi soot', doing bad work was 'snobbin' a job, and a poor workman a 'botherin snob'. Repair work was 'codging' and if anyone told a lie he was 'mogueing' (a 'mogue-hole' is a false button-hole). A tailor was always given his 'crib', that is the trimmings (cloth clippings) and the remains of the silk and button-hole thread left over from the garments he had made. He sold the clippings for making mungo.

All day they sat sewing on the boards and in the evenings crept nearer and nearer to the lamp. Time was passed in long, often political, discussions. When a suit was finished, the older craftsmen would hang it up to admire, and if they found a fault, they rectified it and pressed the suit all over again.

Of the 'whip the cat' tailors, William and Jane Parke of Redmire, Wensleydale, are remembered. Married in 1815, they spent many years travelling from farm to farm. Jane was chiefly engaged in making button-holes. She smoked a clay-pipe and coming from a long-lived family lived to be ninety-three.[1]

Arnold Metcalfe remembers making a special horse dealer's suit for Bill Buck of Appersett, Wensleydale. Made of green tweed the jacket had a yoke with points across back and front, a stitched strap down the back, fancy flaps on the pockets, a big skirt pocket inside, swansdown lining the sleeves, six rows of stitching round the edge of the jacket and round buttons with raised horseshoes in them. In the dales, especially lingering on in Swaledale, breeches and boxcloth leggings were the fashion. Good quality blue serge, twenty-two ounces to the yard, was popular for best suits, gaberdine for overcoats and corduroy for working trousers.

A picture of the sales' side of tailoring comes from Mr Ernest Moore who in 1906 at the age of nineteen started work as a traveller for Oswald Allen, tailor of Hawes, Wensleydale. The business premises still remain occupied by Mr W. Hodgson, draper. At the back of the shop is the cutting room and across a cobbled yard a range of outbuildings with stables for a pony and horse and a trap house; above are rooms with tailors' boards. Besides about five tailors and the London-trained cutter, Allen employed a shirt-maker, Helen Yewdale, working in the same buildings, who earned 1s. a shirt or 1s. 3d. if it had a calico lining. Alloway yarn was also supplied to knitters in Garsdale, mostly elderly women, who from ten ounces of wool knitted men's stockings which came over the knee for 1s. 2d. and from eight ounces shorter ones for 1s.

Ernest Moore spent most of his time travelling round with boxes of patterns and ladies' dresses by horse and trap from Swaledale to Airedale, and each spring and autumn he went by rail to Liverpool where, hiring a horse and trap, he visited the numerous families who had gone there from the dales to find work. He recalls that in his early days a man's suit could be had for 13s. 11d. tailor-made of Scotch Kersey tweed.

[1] Mr R. H. Hunter, Castle Bolton, Wensleydale.

LING THATCHING
& BESOM MAKING

NO doubt in very early days all houses were thatched: and although some straw was once available, ling (heather) was the material in general use in the dales. Thatchers found full-time occupation, and ling for thatching was regularly pulled on heather moors.[1] In the last century many houses, cottages and barns in Colsterdale, Nidderdale, round Barden and Bolton Abbey, Wharfedale, at Hawes, Redmire and Castle Bolton, Wensleydale and in Baldersdale were ling thatched. The last remaining thatches are to be seen near Bowes, Teesdale, and at Hurst, Swaledale, places where ling flourishes.

The principle of thatching with ling partially resembled that of thatching with straw, and slight variations in method occur in the regions where it is remembered. Mr Jonathan Graham, who in 1880 was born at Low Ashhead on the moors between Masham and Nidderdale, has described the procedure in that district as it was taught to him by Tom Rawson, thatcher, on the Swinton estate.

For a start 'good ling ground' with long straight heather had to be found. Gathered between January and April, it was pulled up by the roots by both hands, and about five handfuls were fastened by bands of ling in *loggins* (small battens) of which twenty-four made a *theave*, more usually *threave* (*see plates* 224–7). Some sixty years ago the worker was paid 9d. a theave of which five represented a day's work. Later this rose to 1s. Two hundred to 400 theaves, 'varra near a field full', depending on the size of building were required.

Having brought the ling down by horse and sledge three or four theaves at a time, the thatcher unloosed the bands and was ready to start. His pay, reckoned at so much a theave, was the same as for pulling. Meanwhile the mason had laid a layer of *easings* (flags) on top of the house wall to throw off rain, and the joiner, making a steeply pitched roof, had fixed the spars, often thin straight trees, about fifteen inches apart. The thatcher laid the first layer, roots upward, not quite on the edge, then slanted the next row diagonally. Then the thatcher proceeded in

[1] N. R. *Quarter Sessions Records* vol. 1, Richmond 1609 (William Baitman of Askrigg, thatcher) and P.R.O. E 134 Michs. 6 Anne No 38 York (in 1707 ling pulled for thatching on Harkerside, Swaledale).

courses along the length of the roof, putting two or three rows of ling with one to overlap, keeping the root ends well up and leaving all smooth. Sometimes left partly finished, the thatch had heavy stones laid on it or it was walked on to settle the stiff bushy heather. At the top the thatch might be a yard thick, thicker than at the bottom. After leaving for a time to settle, the gap between the two sides of the thatch at the ridge was bridged by ling wrapped across about a yard wide and alternately laid roots and flower ends.

Lastly, flaughts 2 yds. long by 12 ins. to 15 ins. wide and $1\frac{1}{2}$ to 2 ins. thick, cut with the flaying spade, were rolled up tied with string and carried up the ladder, and were laid across the top overlapping each other about six inches and pegged down by hazel pegs six to a sod, three at each side of the sod. The pegs, 18 ins. to 2 ft. long, were driven in at an angle to prevent water seeping in. The thatch itself was not pegged down, but hazel rods were laid down the sides fastened down by staples made by braying hazel sticks with a mallet and bending them with one end about a foot and the other two feet long with sharpened points. Finally the whole thatch was shaved with an old scythe blade. When it was finished 'It looked a picture'.

In the Barden and Bolton Abbey area a similar method was practised to that at Ashhead, except that small bundles of ling were tied to the spars, set close together, by means of tarred string and a thatching needle, resembling a large darning needle. Thatches no doubt survived here because they were liked by the Devonshires. Gamsworth House, Barden, was the first to be slated. When the then Duchess was driving through, she saw the grey slated roof and ordered it to be re-thatched, which it was by putting the thatch on top of the slates. Many years later it began to slip off and whilst her husband was at market, the then tenant, Mrs Holmes, had the farm men strip it off, and thus the roof remains today.[1]

An account for thatching at West Witton, Wensleydale, in 1711 records $2\frac{1}{2}$d. a threave of ling.[2]

---

[1] Mr C. H. Lister, born at Skyreholme, near Barden.
[2] MS. in authors' possession.

FARM TOOLS AND IMPLEMENTS

1 Horn burn. 2 Face burn. 3 Tup coupling for fastening two tups together by the horns. 4 Pig caumerill. 5 Sheep caumerill. 6 Brand (Metcalfe). 7 Needle for making ling besoms. 8 Besom engine, Ribblesdale (clamp for holding the heather tight). 9 Ladle for running lead when fixing gate crooks in stone. 10 Besom engine (Wharfedale). 11 Moulder for making rake teeth. 12 Stillions (truans). 13 Wool scales (one side may be unhooked to put on the wool sheet). 14 Sheep shears. 15 Thistle stubber. 16 Thraw crook. 17 Cow band of wood, worn with the catch behind the horns. 18 Tar pan and marking iron.

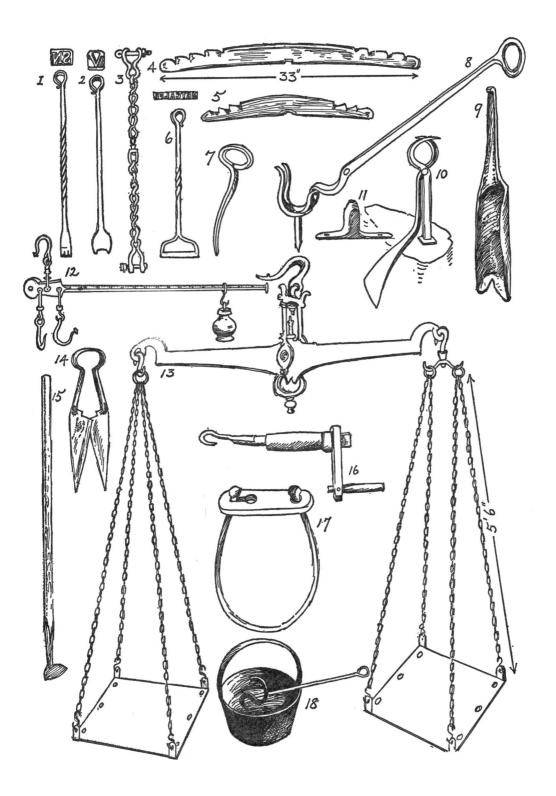

	£	s	d
It. to Oswald Metcalfe for pulling of 94 threave of Linge		18	10
It. to John Richardson & John Furnish for leading the same	1	3	6
It. to John Richardson & Jo: Furnish for leading 4 loads of Easeing stones to Witton		1	4
It. to Also leading sods & stroe, Stephen Ibbison for 17 days Theakeing		19	10
It. to James Plues for serveing theaker 8d per day			6
It. to Rob. Metcalfe 17 days serveing theaker 8d per day		11	4

At Hurst, Swaledale, the ling was pulled in May, tied up in sheaves of which twenty-four made a threave and, left all summer, it was used for thatching at the *back end* (autumn). In winter young hazels were cut to make *spelks*, staples about a yard long which were twisted and bent. Sods were not used for the ridge. The roof consisted of three principals with two rows of purlins to which thin birches were nailed less than a foot apart. The birches had been roughly trimmed so that the snags held the ling. The thatching proceeded in *gangs* (courses) about eighteen inches wide and was held down by spelks placed a similar distance apart. Thatched up to it as tight as possible, the ridge was bridged with heather.[1]

In the summer of 1805 the peat stacks, near the Old Gang Smelting Mills, were being thatched. The rate of 7d. a threave was paid for 393 threaves of ling and the same rate paid for sixty-four yards of thatch. One man led five loads of spelks at 6d. a load, 'to thack the Peats Stacks'.[2]

'Black thack' as it was called shared the same disadvantage of the danger of fire as straw thatch, and in exposed positions there was the considerable hazard of the wind blowing it off. Nevertheless it made a warm roof and lasted twenty or even fifty years without repair or renewal.

Using the same material—ling—besom making was formerly a general craft either practised by the farmer or by men engaged full-time. On good moors hundreds of besom makers were out searching for ling. Some of the best known were the Ibbotsons of Threshfield, Wharfedale, and the last was John Lister (1870–1961) of Skyreholme. Besom making has been well described and we refer the reader to articles by Dr A. Raistrick in *The Dalesman*, vol. XI, and to *Made in England* (1937) by Dorothy Hartley. A saying ran that there were rogues in all trades except besom makers and they put short ends in the middle.

[1] Mr J. J. Robinson, formerly of Hurst, Swaledale.
[2] N. R. County Record Office. ZLB. A. D. Mills Account Book.

HEDGING & STICK MAKING

ALTHOUGH walls form the fences in most of the dales, hedges are general in the valleys round Sedbergh, Dent, Garsdale, Howgill and Cautley. Men who are skilled in walling and hedging, if they commit themselves at all, say that the latter is the more difficult because the material is living and may be killed.

The hedges here, not planted hawthorns but composed of sycamore, hazel, *holm* (elm), ash and briars, have to be laid every five to ten years depending on the quality of the soil, which affects the rate of growth. A good man goes round his farm over these periods, either himself or by employing a professional hedger. Nowadays we are told many farmers do not trouble to learn the art themselves.

The work is undertaken in March when the sap is beginning to rise; and the tools are axes of different sizes, a bush and double-edged saws, a pair of clippers, such as are used in gardens for severing thick branches, and a pair of hedging gloves. The hedger always lays *upbank* (uphill), and if possible towards the sunrise, for the branches spring up that way.

First some of the old *liers* (laid branches) are cut away, and the bottom cleaned out—a boy's job. Then, the new growth is nicked with the axe as low down as possible and the branch laid. One blow is best, but is not always practicable, and the stroke must leave enough of the branch for it to bend without breaking yet not cut off the sap. If branches are *chiggled* (badly cut), they don't live long. 'You mustn't crack the bark, if you want the heads to live.' When laid down the branches are *planted*, woven in and out, with the aim of making a dense even fence. Lastly to hold it from spreading, *gibs* (stakes with a snag left at the top) are driven in about five or six feet apart.

Just as some farmers' sons went on Good Friday to cut hazels in local woods for making handles for home-made besoms, so in late autumn or winter they cut hazels for making walking sticks. Mostly utilitarian sticks for driving cattle or sheep to market, they had a root or bole roughly trimmed with a pocket knife for the handle.

Stick making of late years has become a hobby brought to a fine art either with all-wood sticks or with ones fashioned from wooden shafts and with horn handles

—a method which began about 1910. There is no Yorkshire association or pattern, but the Scottish and the Border Stick Dressers Associations and the Aran type sticks adhere to definite recognizable styles. It is sometimes supposed that like the Border Collies the art of dressing sticks may have been brought to England by Scots drovers.

Although both ash and holly may be used, hazel is most commonly employed, and for an all-wood stick a straight shoot growing from a root or thicker branch from which the handle is fashioned is chosen. For either type the shaft must season for two years before use and it may be straightened in the old style by nailing it when green to a beam or by heating and bending. Finally it is french-polished to give it a gloss.

For the horn handles a ram's horn is boiled to soften it for bending, sawn and rasped into shape, and after fitting it to the shaft, which requires skill, it is beautifully carved with fine chisels and files into any shape which the stick maker fancies—perhaps a trout, woodpecker, fox or buckled strap.

243. *Meet of Bedale Hunt in Leyburn market-place, Wensleydale (early twentieth century).*

244. *Grouse-shooting party on Booze Moor, Arkengarthdale. Left to right: Mr J. Hird, Mr R. Harker, Mr R. Hutchinson, Mr Caygill and Mr J. Whitehead (1890s).*

HUNTING & GROUSE SHOOTING

245. *Mr F. H. Wood, Bolton Abbey, fishing in the Wharfe (February 1963).*

246. *Mr C. Slinger and Mr W. J. Blades, and cowl net, Hawes.*

247. *Mr James Blades (1874–1951), Hawes, Wensleydale, tying flies.*

248. *Italian concertina player and monkey, Settle (date unknown).*

249. *Spaniard and performing bear at Settle (date unknown).*

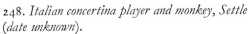

ITINERANTS & MENAGERIE

250. *Wombwell's Menagerie and Bailey's Circus and Museum, Leyburn* (c. *1890s*).

CLUB WALK & BOON DAY

251. *Askrigg Friendly Society, club walk.*

252. *A Boon Day, Howgill Church (1940).*

253. *Children's Sports, Coverdale—Mothers' race (1965).*

254. *Hawes Sports (1966) trotting race. Many of the horses are pacers, with a gait in which the near-side legs move forwards together and similarly the off-side legs.*

SILVER BANDS

255. *Middlesmoor and Lofthouse Silver Band playing at Tan Hill Show (1966).*

256. *Muker Silver Band playing at Arkengarthdale Sports.*

257. *Wallops played at Redmire Feast (26th Sept. 1966).*

258. *Mr Tom Peacock, Reeth, Swaledale, demonstrates how knur and spell was played.*

259. *Having struck the trap with the striker, he prepares to hit the ball thrown into the air.*

260. *Rowleth Bottom Sports, Swaledale (1965). Throwing the quoit standing beside the hob.*

QUOITS   261. *Rowleth Bottom Sports: the quoit flies through the air.*

SPORT & GAMES

FROM the twelfth until about the mid-seventeenth century from Stainmore Forest in the north to the Forest of Bowland in the south vast areas of the dales were preserved for hunting deer. Norman lords and medieval barons alike enjoyed both the sport and the venison. In Elizabethan times deer, fed on hay in winter, were kept in the parks surrounding Middleham Castle. In Stuart times in Craven Sir John Yorke and neighbouring kinsfolk and tenants almost exterminated the deer in hunts prosecuted day after day using guns, crossbows, greyhounds and even pitchforks in a feud with the Cliffords.[1] In Swaledale by 1725 with their browse destroyed by the felling of the woods for lead-smelting, the deer had almost gone.[2]

Sport as part of life in the countryside continued with the hunting of hares and foxes. In the latter half of the eighteenth century the Tempests of Broughton, near Skipton, kept a pack of harriers. Hunting with beagles began later in Wharfedale, Littondale and Ribblesdale, whilst a pack of harriers was at one time based on Kilnsey.[3] The earliest known pack of harriers in Wensleydale was that kept by John Pratt of Askrigg, and as in Craven other small ones proliferated. A pack at Middleham hunting foxes, hares and even the occasional deer, became the nucleus of the Wensleydale hounds, a subscription pack. The huntsman blew his horn at certain points in the dale, and the trencher-fed hounds trotted out from the villages to join him. They hunted hares about three days a week and one day a bagged fox, sometimes even turning to otter-hunting in the River Ure.[4] As was said in the early nineteenth century: 'Our vale possesses a pack of hounds which will follow any animal from a Jack Weazel to an Elephant.'

Horse racing is indigenous. The local gentry, notably in lower Wensleydale and Swaledale, ran horses for cups and sweepstakes on improvised race courses in the seventeenth century and paved the way for what are now important centres of

[1] P.R.O. Star Chamber 8/101/16.
[2] *History of Richmondshire* by T. D. Whitaker (1823).
[3] *Hunting in Craven* by William Gomersal (1889).
[4] *The Wensleydale Hounds Past and Present* by Captain F. Chapman (1907).

training race-horses at Middleham and Richmond. Throughout the eighteenth century saddles, bridles and hats were presented as prizes for horse and also for ass races at Askrigg sports held on the village feast day.[1] In the same century there were Reeth Bridge Races and later, Hurst Races for horses which were *bona fide* property of miners, ore and lead carriers, for which there were besides sweepstakes the prizes of saddles and bridles. Only recently an elderly friend remembered a jockey cap which her ancestors had won for horse racing in Arkengarthdale. Usually after a wedding racing for prizes of ribbons was customary. When Thomas Brown and Ann Coates were married at Muker church, Swaledale, about 1864, seven other couples were married. Afterwards they all rode on horseback for the day to Carperby in Wensleydale, where they raced for red, yellow and blue ribbons.[2]

Racing still continues in the dales in trotting races at Kilnsey Show, Wharfedale and at Bainbridge, Wensleydale, and at Dent and Hawes Sports, now held in fields whereas formerly a road sufficed. The trotter must not gallop and is bred and trained as a pacer, which keeps a gait similar to the ambling palfrey bred in the Middle Ages by the Cistercians.[3]

The extensive moorlands of the dales still serve both as grouse moors and sheep-runs without friction between the two interests. Whitaker states: 'Hawking and netting for grouse was in use to the year 1725, when shooting flying was introduced, to the great astonishment of the dalesmen.' On large estates several game-keepers are employed, besides others working alone for the owners of smaller moors, but their decrease since the First World War has resulted in more vermin than in the past.

Besides shooting foxes, which worry lambs and hens, the keeper sets traps for stoats, weazels and carrion crows, and burns areas of heather, a job undertaken by law only from November to March. In most normal years ideal conditions for burning, with no wind and the ground neither too dry nor too wet, are only experienced for about two weeks, usually in March. Not nearly enough is burnt to keep the moorlands in good order. Grouse sleep in the burnt patches and oddly enough their nests show up less on them than elsewhere. They eat the flowers of rushes, bents and ling which act as a kind of tonic. Traditionally under some employers the keeper is given a brace of grouse after each shoot, a new suit each year and a goose or its equivalent in money at Christmas.

Fishing might be said to be the most popular sport because of the many clear rivers and becks flowing down the dales. All are well stocked with trout and some

---

[1] Yorebridge Grammar School, 'The Book of the Four Men'.
[2] Mr J. Brown (1867–1950) born at Thwaite, Swaledale.
[3] *The Foals of Epona* by A. Dent and D. M. Goodall (1962).

with grayling, while salmon are to be found in certain reaches of most dales rivers, including such small ones as the Clough and the Dee. The Wharfe, where the trout are notoriously shy and the water particularly clear, is regarded as one of the best fishing rivers in the north of England. Each river and even beck contains trout which has its own variant of markings. Captain F. Chapman in *Gun, Rod and Rifle* (1908) recalled that 'forty or fifty years ago when the lead-mines were in full swing, the water of the Swale was so discoloured with lead washings that for not more than one day a week (Monday) was it clear enough for fly fishing.'

A number of dales' rivers contain crayfish which were introduced into the Ure, as recorded in Camden's *Britannia*, by Sir Christopher Metcalfe (1513–1574). In that river they have apparently become comparatively scarce during the last fifty years. Mr W. J. Blades, Hawes, Wensleydale, of the family of that name famous in fishing annals, says that in his father's day as many as 1,000 were caught at a time, and once that number was sent off packed between moss in barrels to stock a Scottish loch.

Formerly fish, usually trout, sometimes minnows, used to be potted. They were cooked slowly in a large dish in the oven in a little water or bacon fat, and when tender were boned and skinned, flavoured with salt and pepper, mixed with butter and reheated before potting.[1] In May 1831 John Dover of Hebblethwaite Hall, Sedbergh, sent off to a relative in London hams, two pots of trout, a small bundle of letters and some oatbread.

In the past poaching was rife in the then remote dales. It was always said of Dent that 'salmon had a one way ticket up the River Dee', and to catch them torches and *leisters* (pronged barbed fish spears) were employed, resulting in catches of sackfuls of salmon. Shackle nets, used in shallow water, came under the jurisdiction of manor courts; poaching nets, made by the local ropemaker, were stretched across the becks round Richmond and fish driven into them. Another weapon for large catches was a *cowl* net, which used in the dusk in flood water was drawn towards the fishermen standing on the bank (*see plate* 246). Piles were sometimes driven into river beds to prevent such netting activities.

Stone-flies (*plecoptera perla maxima*) were formerly regarded as deadly bait. Collected live, they were kept in a cow's horn with holes pierced in it to give air. The horn was closed at the wide end by a well-fitting piece of wood and at the narrow end by a cork which, when a fly was required, was removed. Captain Chapman recounts in his book that using stone-flies he once caught 200 trout in Walden Beck, Wensleydale, between 6 a.m. and 3 p.m.

Spinning, wet fly fishing and clear up-stream worming, 'flying the worm', predominated in the dales' rivers until the 1950's at which time dry fly fishing began

[1] Mrs H. Storey, b. Thwaite, Swaledale.

to become generally popular. Yet in the days of James Blades ('Sproats'), F. M. Walbran, author of *British Angler* (1889), was fishing on the Ure and bet that he could catch fish for fish with his dry fly against James Blades' wet. After that 'Sproats' often tied dry fly patterns. His manuscript book of fly tying patterns and notes is the bible of fishermen on the Ure. Many were his sage words of advice to his grandson, the present Mr W. J. Blades: 'Listen lad,' he would say, 'there are as many fish on this side o' t'river as t'other', meaning don't cast too long a line. Flies tied by W. J. Blades are the most successful on the Ure today. When tying he says, 'Give it plenty of body, less wing, don't have it like a bumble bee'.

Mr F. H. Wood of Bolton Abbey, Wharfedale, who was taught to tie flies by Edmonds, co-author with Lee of *Brook and River Trouting* (1916), says, 'No matter who teaches you something of yourself goes into tying flies.' Very little hackle is required on dales' rivers. A keen fly fisherman, Harry Wood thinks that there is nothing to touch a split cane rod and says that 'your technique should be automatic'.

Besides these country pursuits there were and are the village sports days, a continuation of the religious feasts held on the saints' day of the village church. As we have said horse racing figured at Askrigg feasts, and as at others was combined with foot and fell-races, jumping and wrestling. Formerly all the competitors were local men, but now at a big gathering such as Burnsall Feast in Wharfedale, apart from the children, competitors come from far and wide.

Within living memory, feasts, looked forward to for months ahead, lasted for the better part of a week, and, the only holidays of the year, they were a time for weddings and of reunion for people who had left the dales to seek work and who returned home to visit relatives.

Two well-known feasts are those at West Witton and Redmire in Wensleydale held respectively in late August and late September. The former, remarkable for the custom of the 'Burning of Bartle', is described elsewhere.[1] At Redmire Feast there were formerly dances on five nights of the week, and at one time a pace egg play was given. Men, dressed up, knocking at doors, asked if they could 'oil the clock'—'nothing' we are told 'but an excuse to be given cheesecakes'. Until recently stalls, coconut shies and roundabouts filled the green.

Here, too, wallops were and are still played. Resembling skittles, except that sticks are thrown instead of balls, it is played by men and women but not by children. The men stand on a chalk line about nine yards away from the nine wooden skittles arranged alternately in three rows and the women about six yards off. In the heyday of the feast the prizes for wallops came from the 3d. entry fee.

Gone altogether, except in revivals, are the country dances performed not only

[1] *The Yorkshire Dales* by Marie Hartley and Joan Ingilby (1956, p. 203).

at feasts but fairs. What was the 'old fashioned merry dance' danced at Askrigg June Fair and said to be going out in the 1840's? In two publications Miss L. M. Douglas of Settle printed nine dances of the Yorkshire Dales collected mostly in Wharfedale in the 1930's. Of these 'Square Eight' and 'Six Reel' are known in Wensleydale.

At Muker Awd Roy, Swaledale, possibly a twelfth night celebration, taking place on the Wednesday before Old Christmas Day, 6th January, it was customary for eight or ten men to go round with an apron into which food was thrown and taken to the inns. Seventy years ago stalls exhibited fruit, toys, drapery and knick-knacks, whilst Awd Spice Mary of Reeth crying her wares loudly sold spice loaf and sweets at three halfpence a time. On Thursday outdoor games taking place were *lowping* (jumping), two hitches and three hitches, hipsy-gipsy, cat-gallows (a kind of hurdle race), pole jumping, trotting races and shooting at *loaning* (lane). It was also a time for the general collection of accounts by doctors, badgers and all tradesmen.

Dancing began about six o'clock in an upper room of the Queens Head Inn, lit by candles. The first dance, the Stot dance, was always performed by men only. A favourite was the Wensleydale Gallop, a kind of Sir Roger de Coverley, in which all joined, whilst the grand finale on the Saturday night was the *Whishin* (cushion) dance, Elizabethan in origin. Everyone was seated round the room and when the fiddlers struck up a lively air, a young man led off by bringing a cushion and placing it before his favourite girl. They knelt and kissed. A girl then laid the cushion before her choice and so it went on until all had found partners. If anyone refused to kneel they were gently pushed down with a brush. The couples finally joined arms and tripped round the room singing:

> *Arm in arm, round and round,*
> *Me that loves a bonny lass*
> *Will kiss her on the ground.*[1]

Brass bands were a development of the last century, and before the drastic depopulation of the dales even quite small villages boasted one. It was customary for the members to make rounds at Christmas. Swaledale bands went over to Wensleydale or even into Westmorland. 'Once', said Mr T. Kirkbride, a member of the then Askrigg band, 'we took the train to Aysgarth, played all up Bishopdale, lunched at Cray, then went up to Beckermonds. They hadn't had a band for fifteen years, and they made us all go inside and we played and played. They gave us frumety. My! some o' them bandsmen could eat. You could play well on

[1] Notes dated 1896 by the late T. P. Cooper. The cushion dance was in the reign of Elizabeth I performed at court. See *Dancing* by Lilly Grove (1895).

frumety. Then we walked over by Oughtershaw to Hawes, where about nine o'clock we were met by two wagonettes which took us back to Askrigg.'

Many games in the dales are identical with those played elsewhere, except there may be a dialect word such as *taws* for marbles or *Felt* O (felt means to hide or conceal) for hide and seek in Nidderdale. Taws, whip and top, shuttlecock and battledore for girls, and bools (iron hoops) followed each other in spring. Marbles aroused strong feelings in men and boys who were fain to have some taws; and Irishmen, engaged for hay-time, were known to gamble away their earnings playing them. At Askrigg, Wensleydale, specific names for different games were 'Span Taw, Holey, and Big and Little Ringy', and at the end of the game if a player found that he had the same number of marbles he had started with, he was said to have got his *stonks* (stakes).[1] Bools (pronounced to rhyme with howls) came out at Easter and were blacksmith made. At Malham the boys competed in bouncing them over the stone walls.

A game general in the dales, still sometimes played on outside farms, is described by Mr E. Campbell, who was brought up at Cosh, Littondale. 'We 'ed ter mak our own pleasures. For games we made sheep folds o' bits o' stones and got fir cones— big uns were sheep and little uns were lambs. We used to play for hours. Eh! Mi sister did like it.'

A game played in mid-Wensleydale was Duckies or Coggy on and Coggy off (so called at Preston-under-Scar). Each player had a small stone (a coggy) about as big as a fist. A topstone was taken from a wall and one of the players' coggys placed on top of it. Standing near the big stone, this player was odd man out. The rest, eight or nine yards away, behind an imaginary line, all threw their stones with the object of knocking the coggy off. If they missed the odd man snatched up his stone and as the others rushed to collect theirs and retreat behind the line, he tigged one of them who then became odd man out. He too could tig another contestant before he returned to base.[2]

Two related games were piggy, peggy or guinea pig, played by men and women, and knur and spell, played by men. In the former, the toggle from a cow-band was sharpened at both ends and placed on a flat stone in a field. Sides were chosen. The striker took a stick and struck one end of the guinea which, when it sprang in the air, was hit as hard as possible. Then, judging the distance and the capabilities of a member of the other team, the striker allotted him or her a number of strides in which to reach the guinea. If this was achieved, the opponents received the same number of points as strides. If they failed the striker's side scored.[3]

[1] Mr R. M. Chapman, born at Askrigg.
[2] Mr Jim Peacock, Castle Bolton.
[3] Mr John and Mr Richard Wallbank, born at High Grain, Eldroth.

Mr Tom Peacock, Reeth, Swaledale, possesses the striking stick and trap for knur and spell (wooden ball and trap), and these were used a generation ago at sports at Grinton. Accompanied by betting, it was a popular game with lead-miners, who played at Blades, and from Gunnerside to Ivelet over a course using stiles to cross walls. When struck a spring released on the trap threw a ball in the air and was hit like the 'guinea' as far as possible. The man taking the least number of strokes round the course was the winner. A miners' occupation was sitting whittling pieces of hollywood into balls, rather less in size than a golf ball, which were then whitewashed.[1]

Quoits still figures in the programmes of a few local shows and sports. Once it was played often in the inn yards by enthusiasts night after night throughout the summer, except in hay-time. A set of quoits used to be kept on most farms or failing that the game was played with horseshoes.

To enable two games to continue at once a hob or iron spike is fixed in a square of clay (the box) at either end of the pitch, which is now usually eleven yards but may be as much as eighteen yards long. A match is between two men, playing with two quoits each for eleven up, and is a knock-out tournament. To decide who should start a quoit is tossed up and a player calls out 'ill' or 'owl' (hill or hole), referring to the bevel and the delf on either side of the quoit. The quoit thrown nearest the hob scores one point and if it lands over the hob it is a ringer counting two. Measuring to see which is the nearest should be done by callipers, but often a piece of string suffices.

Playing nightly on the green at Castle Bolton, Wensleydale, the many would-be contestants had to 'poddle in' to decide who played who. A walking stick was laid on the ground and pulling something out of their pockets—perhaps knives or pencils—one man threw them towards the stick and whoever's possessions lay nearest played each other. Games continued until dusk. The last player pitched the quoits into a garden where they were usually kept. At feast times there might be three dozen games of quoits going on over two or three days with four copper kettles as prizes.

[1] The late William Calvert (1900–1965), Gunnerside.

GLOSSARY

of dialect words which appear
in text or captions.

Addle, to earn

Backboard, a scored wooden board used in making oatcake

Backcan, a tin can shaped to fit the back used for carrying milk

Balks, the loft above the cow stalls where the hay is stored

Barm, yeast

Batt, the forward sweep of the scythe when mowing

Beak, a chimney crane at back of kitchen fireplace (term used in Nidderdale)

Bink, a stone bench

Boose, a stall in a cow shed

Bow, a handle

Brot, an overhang of peat hag

Bucket, the spit or spade depth in peat pot (Nidderdale only)

Budget, see *Backcan*

Bukker, a square flat iron hammer

Byelawman, an official in charge of a cow pasture

Cake stool, a three-legged wooden stand for drying oatcake on

Canch, a rectangular layer of hay when cut from the mew (Swaledale only)

Capes, the topstones of a wall (North Riding only)

Chesford, a cheese vat

Chiggle, to chew. To cut wood badly

Clag, to stick

Clapbread, rolled out oatcake

Clapcake, rolled out or formerly beaten out oatcake

Clash, to throw, usually a moist substance.

Clog, a toggle

Closers, the slates of a roof next to the ridge stones

Clots, small broken pieces

Coppy, a stool

Coup, a small cart, either on runners or wheels

Cowl net, a large net with a long handle used to drag fish out of a flooded river.

Cowl-rake, a tool used for scraping either mud from a road or manure out of a cart

Crappins, pork fat rendered down in small pieces

Cratch, a stool for sitting on when clipping sheep

Creel, see *Cratch*

Creels, pair of, bent hazel rods and rope contrivance for carrying hay

Cripple-hole, a hole at the foot of a wall for sheep to pass through (West Riding)

Crow, bars spanning the fire, fixed on front bar of fire grate

Crusie, double oil lamp (Scotland)

Cuddy, a left-handed person

Delf, a hole

Dess, square blocks of hay left after cutting hay in the mewstead

Docken, dock, usually *Rumex obtusifolius*

Doddings, the dirty locks round the tail of a sheep

Dolly, to wash

Double scauping, cracking the frontal bone of a sheep's head

Drinkings, refreshment taken between meals

Fay, the discharge from a festering sore

Felt, to hide

Flaughts, sods

Fleam, a knife used for bleeding animals

Flesh kit, a salting tub

Fodder gang, the passage at the head of the cow stall

Footing, setting up peats to dry. A small pile of peats

Foots, small piles of peats set up to dry

Former, a long rounded wooden stock on which the bows of hayrakes are wedged for bending

Galley-bauk, a bar in the chimney from which a *reckan-crook* is suspended

Gang, a set or course

Gib, a stake with a snag left at the top

Gowdings, see *Doddings*

Gripe, a muck fork

Gripping, open or moor draining

Group, the channel at the foot of the stalls in a cow shed

Hacking, mowing by hand round the borders of a meadow

Haver, from Old Norse *hafri* meaning 'oats'

Haverbread, rolled out oatcake

Havercake, rolled out oatcake

Havermeal, oatmeal

Heaf, pasture ground to which sheep are accustomed

Hebble, a simple form of wooden pack saddle for carrying *backcans*

Heck, shelving

Heugh, see *Heaf*

Hob, small heap, usually of hay

Hoghouse, a shed for young sheep

Holm, elm

How seeds, husks

Hub, small heap, usually of peat

Hull (1) A small covered outbuilding to house animals. (2) Husk. See also *How seeds*

Hut, see *Hub*

Jockey, a haycock

Keds, lice

Kem, to comb

Kemming, an armful of hay, literally meaning a combing

Kist, a chest

Kit, a container for milk

Kitle, an overall-coat

Lapcock, a small haycock

Lathe, a barn

Lea, a scythe

Leister, a pronged barbed fish spear

Lier, laid branches of a hedge

Liggin' grund, literally lying-ground on which peats are dried, usually firm dry ground

Lish, agile

Loaning, a lane

Loggin, a small batten

Lowp, to jump

Mazling iron, an iron bar with a thick ring at end used for treating sturdy in sheep

Mell, a hammer. Harvest supper

Mew, hay in the *mewstead*

Mewstead, the part of a barn where hay is kept

Mistal, a cow shed

Murls, crumbs or dust of peat

Naf, the hub of a wheel

Necessary, a privy

Nib, the handle of a scythe

Nog, peg

Overeasing, large stone flag at eaves of roof

Pike, a large hay cock

Piking, see *Hacking*

Pirn, a twitch used to quieten a horse

Prezzur, the liquid obtained by boiling *keslops*, the dried stomach of a calf

Pricker, a spade used for nicking at the bottom of a spit of peat

Priming kit, see *Flesh kit*

Ramps, garlic

Rated, said of hay spoilt by rain

Reckan-bauk, see *Galley-bauk*

Reckan-crook, a pot-hook

Redwiddie, iron ring on the vertical pole to which cows are tied

Reulling, a supposed remedy for ailing cows in which an irritant was inserted under the skin

Riddleboard, see *Backboard*

Riddlebread, thin oatcake

Riddlecake, rolled out oatcake

Ridstake, vertical pole to which cattle are tied in the stall

Rise, the new wool which lifts the fleece from the skin of a sheep

Round hank, see *Redwiddie*

Rowelling, see *Reulling*

Ruckle, a rick

Rudster, see *Ridstake*

Runner, see *Redwiddie*

Running heaps, a method of gathering up hay with a rake held upside-down

Scale, to spread or strew

Scrapple, a tool used for scraping

Seaves, rushes

Seton, see *Reulling*

Settlestones, the stones at the foot of the stalls in a cowshed

Shade, thin curtain or blind

Sharp, to sharpen a horseshoe for icy road conditions

Shedding, parting in wool of sheep

Shippon, a cow shed

Shools, see *How seeds*

Sinker, the lid of a cheese vat

Sliped, slipped

Slopstone, a shallow stone sink

Smout-hole, a small hole at the foot of a wall

Sooker-stone, the large stone flag above the oven and boiler of a kitchen range forming a flue

Spain, to separate lambs from ewes

Speer, a fixed screen near the outer door

Spelch, stone mason's term meaning to dress a roofing flag to taper off

Spelk, staple used in ling thatching

Spell, see *Closer*, but this term used in West Riding only

Spurn, the bar across the toe of a horseshoe for bad road conditions

Stag, an unbroken and unshod pony

Stamp, a small rick of hay

Statesman, yeoman

Stee, a ladder

Steg, a gander

Stiddy, an anvil

Stock, see *Cratch*

Stonks, stakes in a game

Stoup, stone gatepost consisting of a single upright stone.

Straw-boys and -girls, following the mowers, they strewed the grass by hand

Strickle, a tool for sharpening a scythe

Taws, marbles

Tharve cake, a thick loaf made of whole meal, baked on a girdle

Theave, twenty-four battens, usually of ling for thatching

Thirl-hole, see *Cripple-hole*

Threave, see *Theave*

Thraw-crook, a Scottish term for a tool used for making hay or straw ropes

Titter, to run lightly about

Topping, wool or hair on top of the head of an animal

Traves, shelves supported on stands to hold cheeses

Undereasing, large flagstone at the eaves of a roof

Whangs, leather boot- or shoe-laces

Whinge, to whine

Whishin, cushion

Widdie, see *Redwiddie*

Wisket, container for peat made of plaited hazel

INDEX

Numerals in italics indicate page numbers of drawings. Photographs are indicated by plate numbers at the ends of entries.